International Trade Finance

Gateway to Global market

Aleena Varghese

notionpress.com

INDIA • SINGAPORE • MALAYSIA

Copyright © Aleena Varghese 2024
All Rights Reserved.

This book has been published with all efforts taken to make the material error-free after the consent of the author. However, the author and the publisher do not assume and hereby disclaim any liability to any party for any loss, damage, or disruption caused by errors or omissions, whether such errors or omissions result from negligence, accident, or any other cause.

While every effort has been made to avoid any mistake or omission, this publication is being sold on the condition and understanding that neither the author nor the publishers or printers would be liable in any manner to any person by reason of any mistake or omission in this publication or for any action taken or omitted to be taken or advice rendered or accepted on the basis of this work. For any defect in printing or binding the publishers will be liable only to replace the defective copy by another copy of this work then available.

Table of Contents

Module 1

Introduction to International Trade Finance

Globalisation led to the inter- country barrier- free flow of goods and services which resulted in the economic progress of nations who are interdependent on each other. As the time passed the need for globally accepted financial instruments enhanced to back up the trade transactions.

It is well known that the practice of barter between goods and services among people possesses the history of ages. International trade, however, refers to the exchange of money, goods, and services across international boundaries or regions. Consumer products like televisions and apparel, capital goods like machinery, raw materials, and food are some of the things that are frequently traded. Other transactions involve services, like payments for foreign patents and travel services. Through international trade, nations can widen their markets and obtain goods and services that might not otherwise be accessible locally. The global economy benefits from and is strengthened by this type of trade.

The term "international trade finance" refers to monetary support provided by banks or other financial organizations to importers and exporters using a variety of financial instruments, such as bank guarantees and letters of credit, to enable them to run their business without facing financial strain.

REASONS

There are many reasons why international finance is important and important in today's world. Some of them are:

1. **To understand the impact of globalization on the economy and society**: International finance helps to understand the impact of globalization on the economy and society. Globalization is a process that increases the interdependence and integration of countries through trade, investment, migration, communication and culture.

2. **Cost- benefit analysis on globalisation**: International finance aids in analysing the benefits and costs of globalization, such as economic growth, poverty reduction, environmental impacts, cultural diversity and political stability.

3. **Identifying opportunities and mitigating risks**: Cross-border transactions involve parties from different countries or regions, such as importing and exporting goods and services, investing in foreign assets, borrowing and lending money, and transferring remittances. International financing helps to reduce the risks and opportunities of cross-border transactions.

4. **Assessing risks and rewards:** International financing helps in assessing the risks and rewards of the transactions, such

as exchange rate fluctuations, political uncertainty, legal differences and market imperfections.

5. **Creation and implementation of policies:** International finance is useful in designing and implementing effective policies and regulations for the global economy to guide the behavior and interactions of economic entities such as individuals, businesses, governments and international organizations.

6. **Promotion of global attributes**: International finance can help us shape and coordinate policies and regulations that promote global economic stability, efficiency, equity and cooperation.

FEATURES

International finance is a branch of financial economics that studies how money flows across different countries and regions. Some of the features of international finance are:

1. **Capital Transfer**: International finance allows the transfer of capital from one country to another, such as through foreign direct investment, securities investment, remittances, and foreign aid. It can help countries finance their development, spread risks and access new technologies and markets.

2. **Trade through distribution:** International finance facilitates the distribution of resources and goods between countries through international trade and payments. This can help countries exploit their comparative advantages,

increase productivity and efficiency, and achieve economies of scale and diversity.

3. **Proper use of money:** International finance helps countries manage the supply and demand of money through monetary policy and exchange rate policy. This can help countries maintain price stability, control inflation and balance their external accounts.

4. **Procurement:** International financing involves the procurement of goods and services from foreign suppliers or markets. This can help countries reduce their costs, improve their quality and improve their competitiveness.

5. **Maximizing Investors' Wealth**: International finance provides opportunities for investors to diversify their portfolios and increase returns by investing in foreign assets or markets. This can help investors reduce exposure to domestic risks, hedge currency fluctuations and benefit from better growth prospects.

6. **Cross-border payments:** International finance deals with the settlement of cross-border payment transactions through various payment systems and instruments. It can help countries facilitate trade and investment, reduce transaction costs and ensure the security and efficiency of payments.

7. **International Banking:** International finance involves the provision of banking services across national borders such as deposits, loans, remittances, trade financing and currency exchange. This can help countries access finance, liquidity and credit.

8. **Trade finance**: International finance includes international trade operations such as export credit, import credit, letter of credit, bills of exchange and factoring. It can help countries overcome trade barriers, reduce risks and improve cash flow.

ADVANTAGES OF INTERNATIONAL TRADE FINANCE

International trade helps in fostering a nation in the following ways:

1. **Enables business growth**: The ability to pay suppliers for the delivery of goods or services and the risk of nonpayment are the two fundamental barriers to expansion for any worldwide business.

   Trade financing enables global enterprises to more effectively overcome these obstacles since it offers security on the goods or services that are being exported or imported and is a short- to medium-term working capital method.

   This thus makes it possible for corporate growth.

2. **Ideal utilization of the regular assets of a nation**: The global exchange between at least two countries helps every one of them to make the most ideal utilization of their normal assets. Using these resources, any nation can concentrate on producing goods and services and selling them to other nations to earn currency and strengthen its economy. It likewise assists with keeping away from the wastage of urgent assets and use them to work on the by and large monetary remaining of the country.

3. **Accessibility of various kinds of Labour and products**: One of the significant advantages of global exchange is that it empowers a country to get Labour and products that it can't make all alone because of absence of assets or greater expenses of creation. They can get the goods from outside the country at somewhat lower costs.

4. **Specialization in the creation of specific Labour and products**: A few countries are supplied with specific benefits like regular assets, Labour force, innovation and capital. They are able to produce certain kinds of goods and services with these resources at relatively lower costs and sell them to other nations that require them. They can take part in huge scope creation to take special care of the requirements of home grown as utilization as well as serve the global business sectors. They can also sell large quantities of goods and services to other nations and increase their foreign exchange reserves in return.

5. **Steadiness in costs of items and administrations**: It is one of the significant advantages of global exchange. It assists with figuring out the advantages and shutting down the wild variances that can emerge because of the non-accessibility of these items.

6. **Transfer of technical know-how**: Countries lacking knowledge of production, manufacturing, and technology can gain access to it from other countries through international trade. In addition to boosting their economic prosperity, developing nations can assist underdeveloped nations in the establishment and growth of industries.

7. **Further develop efficiencies concerning creation and dispersion of Labour and products**: Nations can exploit global exchange to expand their size of creation and make it more proficient to take care of the requests of different countries. They can likewise zero in on creating better quality items and administrations while limiting the general expenses.

8. **Advancement of transport and correspondence:** Worldwide exchange between countries can prosper provided that the method for transport and interchanges are powerful and exceptionally productive. Or something bad might happen, it will prompt bottlenecks that can hamper the reasonability of the exchanges. Global exchange frequently goes about as a motivator for countries to work on their transportation and correspondence with different nations to work with the consistent trade of Labour and products.

9. **Further developed relations:** Worldwide exchange between countries likewise prompts a more prominent extent of correspondence between the two countries. It empowers the trading of information and thoughts too. This can encourage more prominent participation and understanding and go about as a foundation for growing more cheerful relations between the two nations.

DISADVANTAGES OF INTERNATIONAL TRADE FINANCE

Even though international trade is helpful in attaining economic growth of a country, but still, it bears some doom

1. **Depletion of Fundamental Materials**

   Worldwide exchange might bring about the weariness of fundamental materials and minerals of a country. A large portion of the minerals were sent out to different nations. Assuming that they had been protected they would have carried better re-visitations of the country.

2. **Influences Homegrown Enterprises**

   The global exchange may unfavourably influence the utilization example of a country because of the import of efficiently produced and on occasion hurtful products. Indian painstaking work experienced an extreme put-off through deregulation and unlimited imports of English material.

3. **Lopsided Economic Development**

   Because of the activity of similar expenses, global exchange prompts specialization and uneven financial improvement which isn't helpful for the thriving of the country.

4. **Evil Effects of Dumping**

   In some cases, certain nations utilize global exchange to dump their products on different nations so as to devalue the worth of the last merchandise.

5. **Reliance on another Country**

   However, it guarantees a better quality of living for a country, it makes the nations subject to unfamiliar business sectors not really for unrefined substances but rather likewise for selling the completed items. It is necessary to lessen or eliminate this dependence.

6. **Against national Defence**

   It is contended that a country which relies upon unfamiliar causes of supply needs protection during the conflict.

7. **Instability and Financial Preparation**

   It is a source of economic instability and it stands in the way of national economic planning for development and growth.

ROLE OF TRADE IN ECONOMIC DEVELOPMENT

1. **Increase in investment:** Businessmen are encouraged to invest more to produce more goods by international trade. As a result, investment rates rise.

2. **Foreign investment:** International trade provides incentives for the foreign investors, besides local investment, to invest in those countries where there is a shortage of investment.

3. **Decrease in poverty:** International trade is crucial to ending global poverty because it provides foreign investors with incentives to invest in countries where there is a lack of investment, in addition to local investment.

International trade additionally helps lower-pay families by offering purchasers more reasonable labour and products. Coordinating with the world economy through exchange and worldwide worth chains helps drive monetary development and lessen poverty locally and internationally.

4. **Market development:** Global exchange plays a significant part in expanding the production of any country. The foreign trade is a remarkable factor in widening the market and encouraging the producers. In nations where the home market is restricted it is important to sell items in different nations.

5. **Inflow of foreign money:** Global trade provides foreign money that is utilized to eliminate poverty and for other useful purposes.

6. **Exchange of Knowledge:** The dissemination of technological knowledge can be facilitated by international trade. A lack of information can be a greatest weakness in the improvement of a nation and this inadequacy can be really eliminated through contact with further developed economies for example by making conceivable through global trade subsequently help in achieving technical and industrial advancement.

7. **Healthy Competition:** By preventing ineffective monopolies and fostering healthy competition, international trade also contributes to economic growth. The more cutthroat an economy is, the more proficient it will be.

8. **Efficient Utilization of means of production:** International trade provides a better ground for productive utilization of different assets because of its similar benefits.

9. **Easy flow of capital:** Worldwide exchange works with short-term and long-term flow of capital between the nations.

10. **Stabilization of prices:** The issue of internal inflation or deflation can be addressed by international trade.

INTERNATIONAL TRADE A BARRIER TO ECONOMY

International trade can frequently hinder the economy in the following ways:

1. **Tariffs:** These are duties paid by homegrown customers on imported merchandise that increment their cost and make them less competitive in the homegrown market. Duties can safeguard homegrown enterprises from foreign rivalry; however, they reduce the consumer choice, lower the living standards, and hinder economic growth.

2. **Quotas:** These are limits on the amount or value that can be imported or sent out. Quotas can guarantee a base degree of domestic production or utilization, yet they likewise make fake deficiencies, raise costs, and create inefficiencies in the market. Smuggling, corruption, and retaliation from trading partners can all result from quotas.

3. **Licenses:** These are permits or approvals expected to import or export certain labour and products. Licenses can manage

the quality, security, or legitimateness of trade; however, they can likewise make boundaries to passage, inflate expenses, and postpone exchanges. Licenses can likewise be utilized as a device of separation or partiality by conceding or denying admittance to certain markets.

4. **Standards:** The characteristics or requirements of goods or services are defined by these rules or specifications. Norms can guarantee similarity, interoperability, or congruence of exchange, yet they can likewise make specialized hindrances to exchange (TBTs) that reject or limit foreign items or administrations. Guidelines can likewise differ across nations or areas, making hardships for dealers to follow various regulations.

5. **Subsidies**: These are monetary or non-monetary help given by legislatures to homegrown importers or exporters. subsidies can improve the intensity, productivity, or reasonability of exchange, yet they can likewise distort the market prices, make unfair advantages, and damage the climate.

INTERNATIONAL TRADE FINANCE

International trade finance refers to the financial support given by banks or other financial institutions using a variety of financial tools, such as bank guarantees, letters of credit, to importers and exporters to enable them to carry out commercial transactions without experiencing financial hardships.

There are different types of international trade finance that can help businesses to carry out commercial transactions across borders. Some of the main types are:

1. **Letters of credit**: These are documents issued by a bank or a financial institution that guarantee the payment of a buyer to a seller, as long as the seller meets the terms and conditions specified in the letter.

2. **Bank guarantees**: These are promises made by a bank or a financial institution to pay a certain amount of money to a beneficiary, in case the applicant fails to fulfil their contractual obligations. Bank guarantees can be used to secure loans, bids, tenders, or performance contracts.

3. **Lending**: This is the provision of funds by a lender to a borrower, who agrees to repay the principal amount plus interest over a period of time. Lending can be used to finance the purchase of goods or services, or to cover the working capital needs of a business. Lending can be secured or unsecured, depending on the collateral offered by the borrower.

4. **Forfaiting**: This is a form of trade finance where an exporter sells their receivables (such as bills of exchange or promissory notes) to a forfaiter (a specialized financial institution) at a discount. The forfaiter then assumes the risk of collecting the payment from the importer. Forfaiting can provide immediate cash flow and eliminate credit and political risks for the exporter.

5. **Factoring**: This is another form of trade finance where an exporter sells their invoices to a factor (a third-party company) at a discount. The factor then collects the payment from the importer and pays the exporter the remaining balance after deducting fees and charges. Factoring can also provide cash flow and risk management services for the exporter.

6. **Export credit**: This is a type of trade finance where an exporter receives financing from an export credit agency (ECA), which is usually a government-backed entity that supports the export of goods and services from their country. Export credit can take various forms, such as loans, guarantees, insurance, or subsidies. Export credit can help exporters compete in international markets and access new customers.

7. **Trade credit insurance:** This is a type of insurance that covers the risk of non-payment by an importer due to commercial or political reasons. Trade credit insurance can protect exporters from losses and enhance their creditworthiness. Trade credit insurance can also facilitate access to other forms of trade finance, such as letters of credit or lending.

PRE-SHIPMENT FINANCE OR PACKING CREDIT

Pre-shipment finance is a kind of funding arrangement that is given to a business before the shipment of goods to the client. It is normally used to meet the expenses of production, like the acquisition of raw materials, labour, and transportation, as well as some other costs brought about before the products are fit to be delivered. Pre-shipment money can assist organizations with dealing with their income and guarantee that they have the fundamental assets to finish their production and shipment plans.

STAGES OF PRE-SHIPMENT FINANCE

The stages of pre-shipment finance are the steps involved in obtaining and using a financing solution before the goods or products have been shipped to the customer. The stages may vary depending on the type and provider of the pre-shipment finance, but generally they include the following:

1. **Identify the need for financing:** The business ought to survey its income circumstance and decide how much and for how long it needs pre-shipment money to cover its creation and commodity costs.

2. **Research and compare lenders:** The business needs to research and look at changed moneylenders, including banks, monetary establishments, or different sources, to find the best pre-shipment finance choices for its requirements. The business should consider factors such as, interest rates, fees, repayment terms, eligibility criteria, documentation requirements, and processing time.

3. **Prepare and submit a loan application**: The business has to prepare and present a credit application to the picked bank, along with the fundamental reports and data. These may incorporate an application form, a firm order or letter of credit from the customer, a license or quota permit for the goods to be exported, a production plan and budget, a cash flow statement, and financial statements.

4. **Review and negotiate the loan terms**: The bank will survey the advance application and direct a credit evaluation of the business. The bank may likewise direct a site visit or examination of the goods to be financed. In light of the assessment, the moneylender will offer a credit proposal with the agreements of the pre-shipment finance. The business ought to survey and arrange the credit terms with the loan specialist until the two parties settle on a commonly satisfactory arrangement.

5. **Sign the loan agreement**: The business ought to consent to the advance arrangement with the moneylender, which will determine the sum, duration, loan fee, charges, repayment schedule, security or insurance, and different agreements of the pre-shipment finance. The business ought to likewise conform to some other customs or necessities forced by the moneylender.

6. **Availability of the loan**: The bank will disburse the credit to the business, either in one single amount or in stages, contingent upon the kind of pre-shipment finance and the creation progress. The business has to utilize the advance sum just for the planned reason for production and shipment of the produced goods.

7. **Repayment of loan**: The business must reimburse the credit sum alongside interest and expenses to the bank as indicated by the concurred reimbursement plan. The reimbursement might be done either from the returns of product deals or from different kinds of revenue. The business likewise needs to give verification of shipment and product reports

to the loan specialist as proof of satisfying its commodity commitment.

REQUIREMENTS FOR GETTING PACKAGING CREDIT

Some of the common requirements for getting packaging credit are:

1. The exporter should have an Import Export Code (IEC) issued by the regional office of DGFT (Director General of Foreign Trade).

2. The exporter should have a confirmed export order or a letter of credit from the customer, specifying the name, quantity, value, and shipment date of the goods to be exported.

3. The exporter should deal with items that are listed under freely exportable goods. If the items fall under the negative list, the exporter should obtain a license to export them.

4. The exporter should submit a formal application form, a production plan and budget, a cash flow statement, and financial statements to the lender.

5. The exporter should agree to repay the packaging credit from the proceeds of export sales or from other sources of income within a specified period.

6. The exporter should provide security or collateral to the lender, such as a pledge or hypothecation of the goods being financed, or other assets.

QUANTUM OF FINANCE

Quantum of finance is the base measure of cash that is expected to begin or support a business, undertaking, or venture. This can rely upon different factors like the nature, size, and extent of the endeavour, the normal returns and dangers, and the accessibility and cost of capital

POST SHIPMENT FINANCE

Post-shipment finance is a kind of funding arrangement that is given to an exporter or dealer after the goods or items have been delivered to the client. It is ordinarily used to overcome any barrier between the shipment date and the payment date, and to work on the income and liquidity of the exporter. Post-shipment money can likewise assist the exporter with relieving the dangers of non-payment, currency fluctuations, and political instability in the buyer's country.

There are various kinds of post-shipment finance, contingent upon the nature and phase of the export process. Some of the normal kinds are:

1. **Purchased/discounted export bills:** This is a sort of post-shipment finance where the exporter sells or limits its product bills or invoices to a bank or a monetary establishment at a limited rate. The bank or the financial institution then gathers the full instalment from the purchaser at a later date.

2. **Advance against export bills for collection:** This is a type of post-shipment finance where the exporter submits its export bills or invoices to a bank or a financial institution

for collection from the buyer. The bank or the financial institution then advances a certain percentage of the value of the export bills or invoices to the exporter, subject to a margin.

3. **Advance against duty drawback receivables:** This is a type of post-shipment finance where the exporter receives an advance from a bank or a financial institution against its duty drawback claims. Duty drawback is a refund of customs duties and taxes paid on imported inputs used in the production of exported goods. The exporter has to submit proof of shipment and export documents to claim duty drawback from the government. The bank or the financial institution then advances a certain percentage of the value of the duty drawback receivables to the exporter, subject to a margin.

RECENT TRENDS IN INTERNATIONAL TRADE

- **The emergence of protectionism:**

In recent years, some countries have taken protectionist measures, such as tariffs, quotas, subsidies, and non-tariff barriers, to limit imports and support domestic industries. These measures are often driven by political, economic, or social reasons, such as national security, trade imbalances, job losses, or environmental issues. However, protectionism can also have negative effects, such as higher prices, lower quality, less competition, and trade conflicts. According to the World Trade Organization (WTO), the number of trade-restrictive measures applied by G20 countries rose by 27% between 2019 and 2021.

- **The expansion of e-commerce and digital trade:**

The fast advancement of information and communication technologies (ICTs) has enabled the growth of e-commerce and digital trade, which refer to the online sale and purchase of goods and services, as well as the cross-border movement of data and information. E-commerce and digital trade offer many advantages, such as lower costs, broader markets, more convenience, and more innovation. However, they also face some challenges, such as cybersecurity, data privacy, consumer protection, taxation, and regulation. According to the UNCTAD, global e-commerce sales reached $26.7 trillion in 2019, accounting for 30% of global GDP.

- **The growing importance of services trade:**

Services trade refers to the exchange of intangible products, such as transportation, tourism, education, health, finance, and entertainment. Services trade has become more important in the global economy, as it adds value, productivity, competitiveness, and diversification. Services trade is also enabled by the advancement of ICTs, which allow the delivery of services across borders through modes such as cross-border supply, consumption abroad, commercial presence, and presence of natural persons. According to the WTO, world services exports amounted to $6.5 trillion in 2019, representing 23% of total world trade.

- **Regional trade agreements:**

Regional trade agreements (RTAs) are treaties that lower or remove trade barriers among a group of countries within a specific region. RTAs aim to promote regional integration, cooperation, and development, as well as to increase market access, lower costs, and create opportunities for trade and investment. RTAs can also serve as building blocks for multilateral trade liberalization and governance. However, RTAs can also cause trade diversion, discrimination, and complexity, as well as weaken the multilateral trading system. According to the WTO, there are 305 RTAs in force as of January 2021, covering more than half of world trade.

- **The impact of global supply chains**:

Global supply chains (GSCs) are networks of production and distribution that span across multiple countries and regions. GSCs enable the breaking up and specialization of production processes, as well as the coordination and optimization of inputs, outputs, and logistics. GSCs offer many benefits, such as lower costs, higher quality, greater efficiency, and more innovation. However, GSCs also involve some risks, such as vulnerability to shocks, disruptions, and uncertainties, as well as environmental, social, and governance issues. According to the OECD, GSCs account for 70% of world trade in goods, and 80% of world trade in services.

METHODS OF INTERNATIONAL INVESTMENTS

International investments are the allocation of funds by an investor, a company, or a government from one country to another country, with the aim of diversifying their portfolio and capturing opportunities in global markets. There are different methods of international investments, depending on the type, purpose, and degree of involvement of the investor. Some of the common methods are:

1. **Foreign Direct Investment (FDI):** This is when an investor acquires a significant stake or ownership in a foreign company or project, and has a substantial influence over its management and operations. FDI can be done through buying the assets of a foreign company, investing in new property, plants, or equipment, or participating in a joint venture with a foreign partner. FDI can provide access to new markets, resources, technologies, and skills, as well as increase the competitiveness and profitability of the investor. FDI can also have positive spillover effects on the host country's economy, such as creating jobs, transferring knowledge, and enhancing productivity. However, FDI also involves higher risks, costs, and uncertainties, such as political instability, currency fluctuations, regulatory barriers, and cultural differences. FDI can also have negative impacts on the host country's environment, social welfare, and national sovereignty, if not regulated and monitored properly.

2. **Financial Instruments:** These are securities or contracts that represent a claim on the assets or income of a foreign company or entity. Financial instruments can be traded on international markets or exchanges, or issued by foreign companies or entities to raise funds from global investors. Some examples of financial instruments are:

   a) **American Depository Receipts (ADRs):** These are certificates that represent shares of a foreign company that are held by a U.S. bank. ADRs allow U.S. investors to buy and sell foreign stocks without dealing with foreign currencies, taxes, or regulations. ADRs are traded on U.S. stock exchanges or over-the-counter markets, and are subject to U.S. securities laws and regulations.

b) **Global Depository Receipts (GDRs):** These are similar to ADRs, but are issued by foreign companies to raise capital from investors in multiple countries. GDRs are denominated in U.S. dollars or other major currencies, and are traded on international exchanges or over-the-counter markets. GDRs are subject to the laws and regulations of the issuing country and the trading country.

c) **Mutual Funds and Exchange-Traded Funds (ETFs):** These are pooled investment vehicles that invest in a diversified portfolio of securities or assets, such as stocks, bonds, commodities, or currencies. Mutual funds and ETFs can be domestic or international, depending on the geographic scope and focus of their investments. International mutual funds and ETFs allow investors to gain exposure to foreign markets and sectors, without having to research and select individual securities or companies. International mutual funds and ETFs can also reduce the risk of investing in a single country or region, by spreading the risk across different markets and economies. However, international mutual funds and ETFs also entail higher fees, taxes, and currency risks, compared to domestic mutual funds and ETFs. International mutual funds and ETFs are subject to the laws and regulations of the countries where they invest and where they are registered.

3. **Multinational Corporations (MNCs):** These are companies that operate in more than one country, and have a global presence and influence. MNCs can be considered as a form of international investment, as they invest in foreign subsidiaries, affiliates, or branches, and generate revenues and profits from their global operations. MNCs can benefit from economies of scale, scope, and learning, as well as access to new markets, resources, technologies, and skills. MNCs can also contribute to the development and growth of the host countries, by creating jobs, transferring knowledge, and enhancing productivity. However, MNCs also face challenges and risks, such as political instability, currency fluctuations, regulatory barriers, and cultural differences. MNCs can also have negative impacts on the host countries' environment, social welfare, and national sovereignty, if not regulated and monitored properly.

INTERNATIONAL MONETARY FUND (IMF)

The IMF is a global organization that was established in 1944 at the Bretton Woods Conference, a meeting of 44 countries that aimed to create a system of international cooperation and stability after the Second World War.

The IMF's main purpose was to oversee the international monetary system, which was based on fixed exchange rates and convertible currencies, and to provide loans and advice to countries that faced economic difficulties or imbalances.

To explain the history of the IMF, we can use a timeline:

1944: The IMF is created at the Bretton Woods Conference, along with its sister organization, the World Bank. The IMF's initial quota, or the amount of money that each member country contributes, is $8.8 billion. The US dollar is the main reserve currency, and its value is fixed to gold. 1947: The IMF begins its lending operations, with France being the first country to receive a loan of $25 million.

1958: The IMF introduces the Special Drawing Right (SDR), a new international reserve asset that can be used to supplement the existing reserves of member countries. The value of the SDR is based on a basket of major currencies.

1971: The US suspends the convertibility of the dollar to gold, effectively ending the Bretton Woods system of fixed exchange rates. The IMF allows countries to choose their own exchange rate arrangements, such as floating, pegged, or managed.

1973-74 and 1979: The world faces two oil shocks, as the price of oil rises sharply due to geopolitical events and supply disruptions. The IMF helps countries cope with the impact of the oil shocks by providing loans and policy advice.

1982-89: The world experiences a debt crisis, as many developing countries struggle to repay their loans to foreign creditors. The IMF coordinates the global response to the crisis, by arranging debt rescheduling, providing financial assistance, and promoting structural reforms.

1990-2004: The IMF plays a central role in helping the countries of the former Soviet bloc transition from centrally planned to market-based economies. The IMF also assists countries that face financial crises in Asia, Latin America, and Africa, by providing emergency loans and policy support.

2005-present: The IMF adapts to the challenges of globalization and the changing landscape of the world economy. The IMF increases its lending capacity, reforms its governance structure, expands its surveillance and analytical tools, and enhances its engagement with emerging and low-income countries. The IMF also responds to the global financial crisis of 2008-09, the European debt crisis of 2010-12, and the COVID-19 pandemic of 2020-21, by providing unprecedented levels of financial and technical assistance to its members.

SDR

SDR is an abbreviation for Special Drawing Rights, which are a kind of international money reserve created and controlled by the International Monetary Fund (IMF). SDRs are not a money, but a right to swap for other money held by IMF member countries. The worth of SDRs is based on a group of five important currencies: the U.S. dollar, the euro, the Japanese yen, the Chinese yuan, and the British pound. SDRs are used for internal bookkeeping purposes by the IMF and some international agreements, and can also be used for lending, borrowing, or paying debts among IMF members.

GOLD STANDARD

Gold Standard is a system where the value of a country's currency or paper money is directly linked to gold. With the Gold Standard, countries agreed to trade paper money for a fixed amount of gold. A country that uses the Gold Standard sets a fixed price for gold and buys and sells gold at that price. That fixed price is used to determine the value of the currency. For example, if the U.S. sets the price of gold at $500 an ounce, the value of the dollar would be 1/500th of an ounce of gold. The Gold Standard is not currently used by any government. Britain stopped using the Gold Standard in 1931, and the U.S. followed suit in 1933, finally abandoning the remnants of the system in 1973. The Gold Standard was completely replaced by fiat money, a term to describe currency that is used because of a government's order, or fiat, that the currency must be accepted as a means of payment.

BALANCE OF PAYMENTS (BoP)

The balance of payments (BOP) is a summary of all the money that a country's residents exchange with the rest of the world in a certain period of time. The BOP includes three main sections: the current account, the capital account, and the financial account. The current account records the trade of goods and services, as well as the income from investments and transfers. The capital account tracks the changes in ownership of non-financial assets, such as land and buildings. The financial account measures the movements of money related to investments, such as stocks, bonds, and real estate. The BOP shows whether a country has a surplus or a deficit, meaning that it earns more or spends more money than it receives from other countries. The BOP also helps the government and other stakeholders to understand the economic performance and potential of a country.

Components of BoP

The components of BoP are the parts of the balance of payments, which is a record of all the money that a country exchanges with the rest of the world in a given period. The components of BoP are:

1. **Current account:** This account shows the trade of goods and services, the income from investments, and the transfers that do not involve assets. For example, exports and imports of goods, tourism, remittances, etc.

2. **Capital account:** This account shows the changes in ownership of non-financial assets, such as land, buildings, natural resources, etc. For example, sale and purchase of property, migration, debt forgiveness, etc.

3. **Financial account:** This account shows the movements of money related to investments, such as stocks, bonds, real estate, etc. For example, foreign direct investment, portfolio investment, loans, reserves, etc.

4. **The current account:** The current account of a nation's balance of payments includes a unilateral transfer account. This account tracks the transfers of money, goods, or services that go from one party to another, with no obligation to repay or reciprocate. Foreign aid, remittances, donations, and gifts are some of the unilateral transfers that occur. These transfers are not the same as trade transactions, which are two-way and require an exchange of value.

Accounting for Bop

The formula for accounting the BoP (Balance of Payments) is:

BoP = Current Account + Capital Account + Financial Account + Balancing Item

This formula shows that the sum of all the economic transactions between a country and the rest of the world should be zero, implying that the inflows and outflows of funds are balanced. However, this is not always the case in reality, and there may be a surplus or a deficit in the BoP. A surplus means that the country receives more funds than it spends, while a deficit means that the country spends more funds than it receives.

The current account tracks the trade in goods, services, and transfer payments. The capital account records the changes in ownership of non-financial assets, such as patents, trademarks, etc. The financial account shows the net borrowing and lending of a country with the rest of the world. The balancing item is a statistical adjustment to account for any errors or omissions in the data.

Current account deficit and its causes

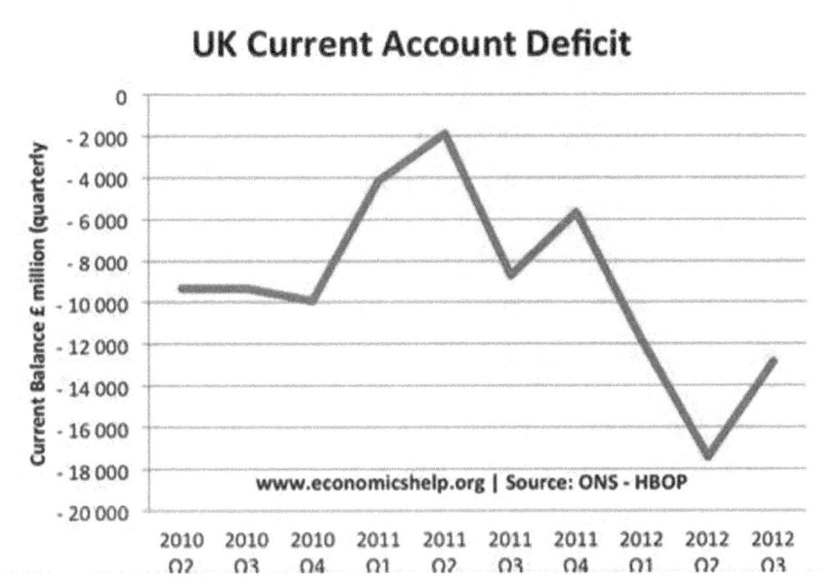

The current account deficit has two types of causes: long-term and short-term. Long-term causes are linked to the country's economic characteristics, such as how industrialized, productive, inflationary, and competitive it is. Some long-term causes of a current account deficit are:

- A high exchange rate, which makes exports less affordable and imports more attractive, lowering the net export income.

- A low level of industrialization, which restricts the variety and quality of products that can be exported, and makes the country depend more on imported materials and goods.

- A high inflation rate, which reduces the value of the domestic currency and makes domestic goods and services less competitive.

- A low level of research and development, which limits the innovation and diversification of the export sector, and exposes it to cheaper competition from other countries.

Short-term causes are related to the changes in the economic activity, such as the income, spending, saving, and borrowing. Some short-term causes of a current account deficit are:

- A high level of consumer spending, which increases the demand for imported goods and services, especially if the domestic production cannot meet the domestic demand.

- A low level of domestic saving, which reduces the availability of capital for investment and production, and increases the reliance on foreign borrowing.

- A high level of foreign borrowing, which increases the net income payments to foreign lenders, and adds to the current account deficit.

- A recession in other countries, which reduces the demand for the country's exports, and lowers the export earnings

Effects of current account deficit

- A current account deficit may have some short-term benefits, but it can harm the economy in the long run.

- The international market loses interest in the country's products and assets (such as government bonds) and the country's currency becomes weaker compared to other currencies. This makes the assets cheaper in the foreign investors' currency, which is getting stronger. This lowers the demand for the country's assets even more. This may trigger a point where investors will sell the assets at any cost.

- The country owns some foreign assets that are valued in foreign currency. When the country's currency drops, the foreign assets become more valuable, which helps reduce the current account deficit.

- A weaker currency should boost exports, as the goods and services are more affordable.

- Imports should decrease, as foreign goods and services become more expensive due to inflation. These trends should balance out any current account deficit.

- The current account deficit leads to either a sudden or a gradual fall in the currency value, which reduces the living standards of the domestic population.

Negative Effects of Current Account Deficit

- A current account deficit can be financed by borrowing from abroad. But this means paying interest on the loans later.

- The international business and financial community will judge the country harshly for having continuous current account deficits. They will doubt the country's ability to repay its foreign debts. Investors will stay away from a weak economy. In this situation, foreign countries will not lend money to the domestic country, making it hard to cover the current account deficits.

- The currency value will go down.

- The domestic economy will be exposed to the fluctuations of international business cycles and interest rates.

- The country may have to increase interest rates to draw more foreign investment and to maintain a certain exchange rate.

- Selling domestic assets to foreigners will result in outflow (as incomes, dividends are sent to their home country), which will worsen the current account deficit even more.

- Higher interest rates will have a deflationary effect on the domestic economy.

- The funds coming in on the capital account may be based on speculation, which means the recipient country is in trouble.

- There is a risk of foreign capital leaving- if this happens, the domestic economy will face higher unemployment as capital departs and imports drop sharply.

Current Account Deficit - Indian Situation

"India spends more on imports than it earns from exports, which means it has a current account deficit. The Reserve Bank of India reports the current account deficit in India. The current account deficit in India shrank to 6200 USD Million in the second quarter of 2015 from 7800 USD Million a year before. Imports dropped more than exports because of lower oil prices, which led to a smaller trade deficit. The current account deficit for the three months to June of 2015 was equal to 1.2 percent of the country's GDP. The Reserve Bank of India data showed that the measure decreased to 1.2 per cent of gross domestic product, or $6.2 billion, from 1.6 per cent, or $7.8 billion, a year before. "The main reason for this improvement was the merchandise trade deficit of $34.2 billion during Q 1 which shrank on a year-on-year basis because of a bigger drop in merchandise imports than merchandise exports," said RBI.

Current Account in India had an average of -1722.32 USD Million from 1949 to 2015, reaching a peak of 7360 USD Million in the first quarter of 2004 and a lowest point of -31857.20 USD Million in the fourth quarter of 2012."

Methods of Correcting Current Account Deficit

Current account deficit is an imbalance in the balance of payments that requires economic policy adjustments.

- **Short run policies:** by interfering in the market to make domestic goods cheaper than imported goods-adopt protectionist measures to reduce import expenditure, the deficit is fixed.

- **Long run policies:** improving domestic competitiveness i.e. boosting R&D, productivity and bringing in innovation, technology and quality enhancement methods etc.

Policies to Reduce A Current Account Deficit

1. Devaluation

Lowering the value of the currency compared to others. (For example, selling pounds in the international market would make the Pound drop)

- If the currency is devalued, the cost of importing goods rises and so the quantity demanded of imports declines.

- Exports will be more affordable and there will be a rise in the quantity of exports.

- Therefore, if demand is relatively responsive to price changes; we would expect a devaluation to improve the current account.

The Marshall Lerner Condition

The Marshall-Lerner condition, which says that a currency devaluation will only improve the balance of payments if the total of demand elasticity for imports and exports is more than one, is named after English economist Alfred Marshall (1842-1924) and the Romanian born economist Abba Lerner (1905 - 1985).

- If (PED x + PED m > 1) then a devaluation will improve the current account.

- If (PED x + PED m > 1) then an appreciation will worsen the current account.

This is because the effect on the current account depends on the total value and not just the quantity of exports.

The J Curve effect

When a country's currency loses value, its current account balance will follow a J-curve pattern. At first, the country'stotal   v a l u e of exports (goods sold abroad) is less than its total value of imports (goods bought from abroad) leading to a current account deficit. The currency devaluation makes its exports cheaper. As a result, the country's level of exports slowly improves, and the country's deficit turns into a trade surplus.

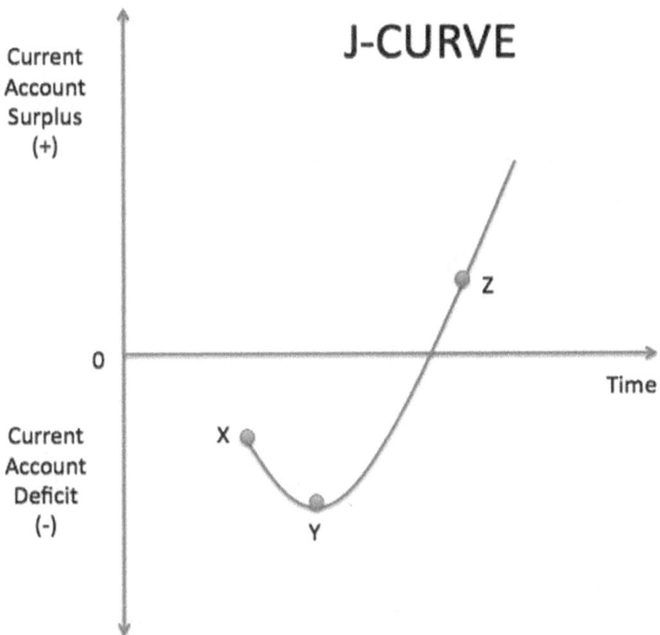

Right after the currency becomes weaker or devalued, the amount of imports and exports may stay the same because of existing trade agreements that have to be fulfilled. (In the short run, demand for the pricier imports and demand for exports, which are more affordable to foreign buyers using foreign currencies stay price inelastic.)This is because of delays in the consumer's search for suitable, cheaper alternatives. (This may not happen).

But in the long run, the exchange rate decline can have the intended effect of enhancing the current account balance. Domestic consumers may switch their spending to domestic products, instead of costly imported goods and services (assuming similar domestic options exist). Likewise, many foreign consumers may switch to buying the products being exported into their country, which are now cheaper in the foreign currency, rather than their own locally produced goods and services.

2. Deflation

If a government lowers aggregate demand by increasing interest rates or taxes then people will have less money to spend and they will buy fewer imports. Deflationary policies will also force manufacturers to cut costs and this will make exports more competitive and so exports will rise. But this policy will clash with other macroeconomic goals like with lower Aggregate Demand, growth will drop causing more unemployment. A government is not likely to want to face more unemployment just to improve a current account deficit.

Supply side policies can boost the economy's competitiveness and make exports more appealing. This can enhance the current account situation, but it may take a long time to work. Some of the supply side policies are described below:

1. Making suitable changes in the taxation to support the supply side. This usually means lowering direct tax rates, such as income and corporation tax. Lower income tax will

motivate unemployed workers to enter the labor market, or for existing workers to work more. Lower corporation tax will encourage unemployed workers to enter the labor market, or for existing workers to work more. Lower corporation tax will also inspire entrepreneurs to start and thus increase national output.

2. Other supply-side policies involve the encouragement of more competition in labor markets, by eliminating restrictive practices, and labor market barriers.

3. Actions to improve labor mobility will also have a positive impact on labor productivity, and on supply-side performance. This increases labor market flexibility.

4. Improved education and training to enhance skills, flexibility, and mobility also known as human capital development. Spending on education and training will likely improve labor productivity and is a vital supply-side policy choice, and one preferred by recent governments across the world. A government may spend money directly, or offer incentives for private providers to join the market. Governments may also establish and oversee standards of teaching, and compel schools to include a skills element in their curriculum.

5. The introduction of performance-related pay in the public sector is also seen as an option for the government to help improve overall productivity.

6. Government can promote local rather than central pay bargaining. National pay rates seldom reflect local conditions, and lower labor mobility. For instance, national

pay rates for Postmen do not show the fact that in some areas they may be scarce, while in other areas there may be excess. Having different rates would allow labor to move to where it is most needed.

3. Protectionism

Protectionism is a set of policies used to shield domestic industries from foreign rivals by imposing taxes or limits on imports. Higher tariffs or quotas will lower imports and enhance the current account. But Protectionism causes backlash from your foreign competitors and leads to a drop in the country's exports.

Policies to reduces current account deficit

The current account deficit has different impacts, which can be good or bad, depending on the country's situation and viewpoint. Some of the potential impacts are:

1. **Weaker currency:** A current account deficit shows that the country imports more than it exports, which means that there is less demand for its currency than supply. This can cause the currency to lose value, which can make exports more attractive and imports more costly. This can help lower the current account deficit over time, as well as boost domestic production and employment. However, a weaker currency can also raise the price of foreign debt, inflation, and imported goods, which can harm the economy and the people's welfare.

2. **Higher interest rate:** A current account deficit indicates that the country borrows from abroad to fund its overspending,

which increases its foreign debt and its net payments to foreign lenders. This can make the country more exposed to changes in the global financial markets, such as an increase in the interest rates or a loss of trust by the lenders. To draw foreign capital and keep its solvency, the country may have to increase its domestic interest rate, which can deter investment and consumption, and slow down economic growth. However, a higher interest rate can also promote saving and lower inflation, which can improve the balance of payments and the budget situation of the country.

3. **Change of ownership**: A current account deficit suggests that the country sells more assets than it buys, which means that the foreigners have a growing stake in its resources and income. This can lead to a loss of economic independence and power, as the country becomes more reliant on the decisions and policies of the foreign investors and creditors. The country may also lose some of its strategic and valuable assets, such as natural resources, technology, and infrastructure, which can reduce its long-term growth potential and competitiveness. However, a change of ownership can also bring advantages, such as access to foreign capital, technology, and markets, which can improve the productivity and efficiency of the economy.

Bank for International Settlements (BIS)

Bank for International

Settlements is an international financial institution that promotes collaboration among central banks and supports global monetary and financial stability. The BIS also offers banking services, but only to central banks and other international organizations.

Some of the roles and activities of the BIS in international trade are:

1. Creating and applying international standards and best practices for banking regulation, supervision, and risk management, such as the Basel Accords.

2. Doing research and analysis on global economic and financial issues, such as trade, capital flows, exchange rates, inflation, and financial stability.

3. Encouraging dialogue and consultation among central banks and other authorities on monetary policy, financial regulation, and international cooperation.

4. Providing a platform for the settlement of international payments and the management of foreign exchange reserves.

5. Serving as a lender of last resort for countries facing financial crises or liquidity shortages.

World Trade Organization (WTO)

The WTO is the World Trade Organization, which is an international organization that handles the rules of trade among countries. Its main objective is to ensure that trade moves smoothly, fairly, and freely around the world. The WTO was established in 1995, replacing the General

Agreement on Tariffs and Trade (GATT), which had been operating since 1948. The WTO has 164 members, representing over 98% of global trade and global GDP. The WTO's

headquarters is in Geneva, Switzerland, and its current Director-General is Ngozi Okonjo-Iweala from Nigeria. Some of the things that the WTO does are:

- It offers a platform for countries to negotiate and sign trade agreements, which usually aim to lower or remove tariffs, quotas, and other trade barriers.

- It oversees and enforces the execution of these agreements, and assists countries in settling trade disputes through its dispute settlement system.

- It performs research and analysis on global trade issues, such as trade and development, trade and environment, trade and health, etc.

- It collaborates with other international organizations, such as the United Nations, the World Bank, and the International Monetary Fund, to tackle the challenges and opportunities of globalization.

COMPONENTS OF INTERNATIONAL FINANCIAL SYSTEM

The international financial system has four main components:

- **The foreign exchange market**: Foreign exchange market which is the market where currencies are exchanged and their prices are set. The foreign exchange market is a decentralized market, meaning that there is no central place or authority that controls the transactions. The foreign exchange market is affected by various factors, such as supply and demand, interest rates, inflation, trade flows, and political events.

- **The currency convertibility**: Currency convertibility is the extent to which a country's currency can be easily traded for other currencies or gold. Currency convertibility impacts the convenience and cost of international trade and investment, as well as the stability and trustworthiness of a country's monetary policy. Some countries put limits on currency convertibility, such as capital controls, tariffs, quotas, or countertrade, to safeguard their domestic economy or balance of payments.

- **The international monetary system**: International monetary system which is the set of rules and institutions that regulate the international payments and transfers related to current and capital transactions. The international monetary system also decides the availability and distribution of international reserves, which are the assets that countries use to pay their international obligations. The main institutions of the international monetary system are the International Monetary Fund (IMF) and the Bank for International Settlements (BIS), which offer financial support, policy guidance, and regulatory supervision to the member countries.

- **The international financial markets**: International financial markets which are the markets where financial assets, such as stocks, bonds, derivatives, and commodities, are traded across borders. The international financial markets offer opportunities for diversification, risk management, and arbitrage, as well as sources of funding and investment for individuals, firms, and governments. The international financial markets are also influenced by various factors, such as interest rates, exchange rates, inflation, economic growth, and political events

Features of International trade system

The internal trade system has these characteristics:

- Includes transactions among the producers, consumers, and the middlemen, such as wholesalers and retailers, who help distribute goods and services.

- Uses the currency of the domestic country as the means of payment, which avoids the risk of exchange rate changes and currency convertibility problems.

- Follows the laws, regulations, and policies of the domestic country, which may apply taxes, tariffs, quotas, or other limits on the movement of goods and services.

- Has two kinds of trade: wholesale trade and retail trade. Wholesale trade is the selling of goods and services in large amounts to other traders or intermediaries, who then sell them to the final consumers. Retail trade is the selling of goods and services in small amounts directly to the final consumers.

- Has different types of retailing, such as fixed shop, chain store, mail order, consumer cooperative, and supermarket, which vary in their location, size, ownership, and way of operation.

WORLD BANK

The World Bank is the common name for two of the five institutions that form the World Bank Group: The International Bank for Reconstruction and Development (IBRD) and the International Development Association (IDA). The IBRD lends to countries that have a moderate- or high-income level, while the IDA lends to countries that have a low-income level or face special challenges. The other three institutions are the International Finance Corporation (IFC), the Multilateral Investment Guarantee Agency (MIGA), and the International Centre for Settlement of Investment Disputes (ICSID), which concentrate on the private sector and investment issues.

The World Bank was established in 1944, together with the International Monetary Fund (IMF), at the Bretton Woods Conference, which aimed to create a new international economic order after World War II.

The initial purpose of the World Bank was to help reconstruct the war-damaged countries of Europe and Asia, and later to support the development of the newly independent countries in Africa, Asia, and Latin America. Over the years, the World Bank has broadened its scope and activities to address various global challenges, such as poverty, inequality, climate change, health, education, gender, and governance.

IBRD

The IBRD is the common name for two of the five institutions that form the World Bank Group: The International Bank for Reconstruction and Development (IBRD) and the International Development Association (IDA). The IBRD lends to countries that have a moderate- or high-income level, while the IDA lends to countries that have a low-income level or face special challenges. The other three institutions are the International Finance Corporation (IFC), the Multilateral Investment Guarantee Agency (MIGA), and the International Centre for Settlement of Investment Disputes (ICSID), which concentrate on the private sector and investment issues.

The IBRD was established in 1944, together with the International Monetary Fund (IMF), at the Bretton Woods Conference, which aimed to create a new international economic order after World War II. The initial purpose of the IBRD was to help reconstruct the war-damaged countries of Europe and Asia, and later to support the development of the newly independent countries in Africa, Asia, and Latin America. Over the years, the IBRD has broadened its scope and activities to address various global challenges, such as poverty, inequality, climate change, health, education, gender, and governance.

Module 2

Letter of Credit

IRREVOCABLE LETTER OF CREDIT

(On Bank or Lending Institution Letterhead)

TO: City of Greenacres
5985 10th Avenue North
Greenacres, Florida 33463

Attn.: Director of Engineering

Letter of Credit No. : _______________

Date: ________________________________

Gentlemen:

This is to advise that ___________________________________, hereby extends its irrevocable
(Bank or Lending Institution)
credit to the City of Greenacres of Palm Beach County, Florida, in the sum of _____________

___________________________________ dollars to guarantee that all improvements set

forth in the ____ Subdivision Plans and
(name of subdivision)
Specifications, as approved by the City of Greenacres, will be fully completed and paid for by

___________________________. Developer of said Subdivision pursuant to the Contract
(name of developer)
for Construction of Required Improvements.

The ___________________________________, guarantees that this sum shall be
(Bank or Lending Institution)
available upon demand by the City of Greenacres, available by your drafts at sight, along
with your signed statement that drawing is due to the Developer's default or failure to
perform by the ________ day of _____________________, 20 ____, all improvements set forth

in the ___________________________ Subdivision Plans and Specifications.
(name)
In the event that the improvements shown on the Subdivision Plans and Specifications are
not completed or paid in full by the ________ day of _____________________, 20 ____, then
and in that event, the City of Greenacres, Florida is authorized to draw upon this credit.

You will notify us when either:

1.   The improvements have been timely completed and the credit may be released,
or

2.   The Developer has failed to perform or is in default on its obligation to
complete and pay for said improvements.

A letter of credit, or "credit letter," is a letter from a bank ensuring that a buyer's payment to a seller will be settled on time and for the right sum. If the buyer can't make the payment, the bank will be expected to cover the full or remaining part of the purchase.

The following are the main characteristics of a letter of credit.

1. **Negotiability**

    A letter of credit is a conditional arrangement, under which the terms can be adjusted/changed at the party's consent. In order to be negotiable, a letter of credit should incorporate an unconditional promise of payment upon demand or at a particular point in time.

2. **Revocability**

    A letter of credit can be revocable or permanent. Since a revocable letter of credit can't be affirmed, the obligation to pay can be repudiated at any time. In an irreversible letter of credit, all the parties hold power, it can't be changed/adjusted without the concurred consent of the related parties.

3. **Transfer and assignment**

    A letter of credit can be transferred, likewise, the beneficiary has the privilege to transfer/assign the LC. The LC will stay effective regardless of how frequently the beneficiary transfers/assigns the LC.

4. Sight and Time drafts

In this type of letter of credit, the beneficiary will be paid by the issuing bank only after furnishing the necessary documents.

5. Commercial letter of credit

A Commercial letter of credit (CLC) is a bank-issued document that guarantees a supplier to a company compensated for the goods and services it gives. The organization might demand a CLC from the responsible bank when one of its providers is uncertain about his capacity to pay.

Purpose of issuing export letter of credit

A letter of credit is beneficial for both the buyer and seller as it ensures the seller that he will receive his money upon the accomplishment of terms and conditions of the trade agreement and the buyer can depict his financial soundness and negotiate the payment terms. The letter of credit may be received for following purpose:

- For physical export of goods and services from India to a Foreign Country.

- For sale of goods by Indian exporters with total procurement and supply from outside India. In all the above cases there would be earning of Foreign Exchange or conservation of Foreign Exchange.

- For execution of projects outside India by Indian exporters by supply of goods and services from Indian or partly from India and partly from outside India.

- Banks in India associated themselves with the export letters of credit in various capacities such as advising bank, confirming bank, transferring bank and reimbursing bank.

- Towards deemed exports where there is no physical movements of goods from outside India But the supplies are being made to a project financed in foreign exchange by multilateral agencies, organization or project being executed in India with the aid of external agencies.

Importance of Letter of credit

A Letter of credit is important to both the buyer and the seller in the following ways:

1. Letter of credit advantages for the seller

- The seller has the assurance of the buyer's banks to pay for the shipped goods.

- decreasing the production risk, if the buyer revokes or changes his order.

- The opportunity to get financing in the period between the shipment of the goods and receipt of payment (especially, in case of deferred payment).

- The seller is able to calculate the due date for the goods.

- The buyer cannot refuse to pay due to a complaint about the goods.

2. Letter of credit advantages for the buyer

- The bank will pay the seller for the goods, on condition that the latter submits to the bank the pre- agreed documents in line with the terms of the letter of credit.

- The buyer can control the time period for shipping of the goods.

- By a letter of credit, the buyer represents his solvency.

- In the case of issuing a letter of credit providing for delayed payment, the seller grants a credit to the buyer.

- Providing a letter of credit allows the buyer to avoid or reduce pre- payment.

Parties in Letter of credit

Applicant: An applicant (buyer) is a person who requests his bank to issue a letter of credit.

Beneficiary: A beneficiary is basically the seller who receives his payment under the process.

Issuing bank: The issuing bank (also called an opening bank) is responsible for issuing the letter of credit at the request of the buyer.

Advising bank: The advising bank is responsible for the transfer of documents to the issuing bank on behalf of the exporter and is generally located in the country of the exporter.

Other parties involved in an LC arrangement:

Confirming bank: The confirming bank provides an additional guarantee to the undertaking of the issuing bank. It comes into the picture when the exporter is not satisfied with the assurance of the issuing bank.

Negotiating bank: The negotiating bank negotiates the documents related to the LC submitted by the exporter. It makes payments to the exporter, subject to the completeness of the documents, and claims reimbursement under the credit.

Reimbursing bank: The reimbursing bank is where the paying account is set up by the issuing bank. The reimbursing bank honours the claim that settles the negotiation/acceptance/payment coming in through the negotiating bank.

Second Beneficiary: The second beneficiary is one who can represent the original beneficiary in their absence. In such an eventuality, the exporter's credit gets transferred to the second beneficiary, subject to the terms of the transfer.

Types of Letter of credit

The following are the main types of letter of credit prevailing in the market

1. **Irrevocable LC:** An irrevocable letter of credit (ILOC) is an authentic correspondence from a bank that assures payment for goods or services being acquired by the individual or entity, referred to as the applicant, that requests the letter of credit from an issuing bank.

2. **Revocable LC:** A revocable letter of credit is one which can be cancelled or amended by the issuing bank at any time and without prior notice to or consent of the beneficiary.

3. **Stand-by LC:** This LC is nearer to the bank assurance and offers more adaptable cooperation chance to Seller and Buyer. The Bank will honour the LC when the Buyer fails to fulfil payment liabilities to Seller.

4. **Confirmed LC:** In addition to the bank assurance of the LC issuer, this LC type is affirmed by the seller's bank or some other bank. Regardless to the payment by the Bank giving the LC (guarantor), the Bank affirming the LC is liable for the execution of commitments

5. **Unconfirmed LC:** Only the LC issuing bank will be liable for payment of this LC.

6. **Transferable LC:** This LC empowers the seller to apportion a part of the letter of credit to different parties. This LC is particularly useful in those situations when the seller is certainly not a sole producer of the products and buys some parts from other parties, as it eliminates the need to open new LCs for different parties.

7. **Back-to-Back LC:** This LC type requires issuing a second LC based on the main letter of credit. LC is opened for the mediator according to the buyer's directions and based on this LC and guidelines of the middle person another LC is opened for the seller of the products.

8. **Payment at Sight LC:** According to this LC, payment is made to the seller immediately (maximum within 7 days) after furnishing the required documents.

9. **Deferred Payment LC:** According to this LC the payment to the seller is not made when the documents are submitted, but instead at a later period defined in the letter of credit. In most cases the payment in favour of Seller under this LC is made upon receipt of goods by the Buyer.

10. **Red Clause LC:** The seller can demand an advance of the agreed LC amount before shipment of goods and submittal of required records. This red clause is so named on the grounds that it is generally imprinted in red to draw attention to notice the "advance payment" term of the credit.

11. **Revolving letter of credit:** A revolving letter of credit is a single letter of credit that covers multiple transactions over a long period of time. It is very specific in a way that is used for regular shipments of the same items between the same buyer(importer) and the seller (exporter).

Documents required for a Letter of Credit

- Bill of Lading

- Airway Bill

- Commercial Invoice

- Insurance Certificate

- Certificate of Origin

- Packing List

- Certificate of Inspection

Export Operations Under Letter of credit

Export Letter of Credit is issued for a trader for his purchase of goods and services. The operations under issuing an export Letter of credit are follows:

1. **Advising an Export LC**

   The essential obligation of an advising bank is to advise the credit received from its abroad branch subsequent to checking the clear validity of the credit recognised by the responsible bank. It is additionally fundamental for the advising bank to go through the letter of credit, understand the underlying transaction, terms and conditions of the credit and advise the beneficiary in the matter.

   The main features of advising export LCs are:

   1. There are no credit risks as the bank receives a one time commission for the advising service.

   2. There are no capital adequacy needs for the advising function.

2. **Advising of Amendments to L/Cs**

   Amendments can be made to an LCs for a number of reasons, but it is necessary to follow all the necessary the procedures outlined for advising. Amendments will be done only on the receipt of satisfactory information/

clarifications. The Issuing bank serializes the amendment number in the process of advising the amendments and also ensures that no previous amendment is missing from the list.

3. Confirmation of Export Letters of Credit

In addition to the confirmation of the issuing bank, the confirmation constitutes a definite undertaking of the confirming bank which takes care of the sight payment, deferred payment, acceptance or negotiation.

Banks in India have the facility of mitigating the credit confirmation risks with Export Credit Guarantee Corporation (ECGC) under their "Transfer Guarantee" scheme and include both the commercial and political risk involved.

4. Discounting/Negotiation of Export LCs

When the exporter requires funds before due date then he can discount or negotiate the LCs with the negotiating bank. Once the issuing bank nominates the negotiating bank, it can take the credit risk on the issuing bank or confirming bank.

However, in such a situation, the negotiating bank bears the risk associated with the document that sometimes arises when the issuing bank discover errors or defects in the documents and refuses to honour its commitment on the due date.

5. Reimbursement of Export LCs

On the receipt of recommendation of issuing bank, the reimbursing bank allows the negotiating bank to collect the money from the reimbursing bank once the goods have been shipped. It is quite similar to a cheque facility provided by a bank.

In return, the reimbursement bank receives a commission on transaction and enjoys float income without paying much involvement in checking the transaction documents. reimbursement bank plays an important role in payment on the due date (for usance LCs) or the days on which the negotiating bank demands the same (for sight LCs).

Import Letter of Credit

An Import Letter of Credit is a financial instrument by the issuing bank that guarantees payment to the exporter on behalf of an importer, provided the terms and conditions specified in the Letter of Credit have been fulfilled.

A bank issue an import letter of credit on the behalf of an importer or buyer under the following Circumstances:

- When an importer is importing goods intra- nation.

- When a trader is purchasing goods from own country and sells it to another country for the purpose of merchandising trade.

- When an exporter who is executing a contract outside his own country requires importing goods from another country to the country where he is executing the contract

Working of a letter of credit

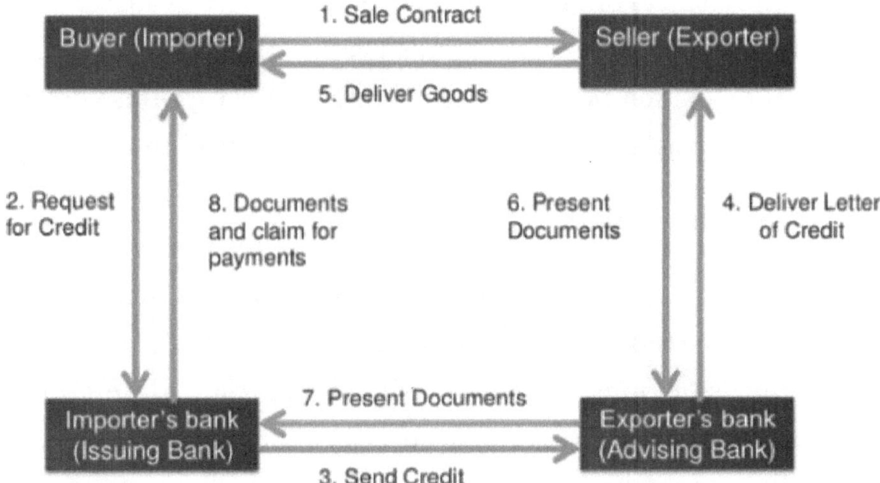

Risks associated with opening import Letter of Credit

The basic risk associated with an issuing bank while opening an import LC are:

1. The financial standing of the importer

As the bank is responsible to pay the money on the behalf of the importer, thereby the bank should make sure that if the importer has the proper funds to pay back.

2. The goods

The banks should conduct a detailed analysis against the risks associated with durability of the goods, chances of obsolescence, import regulations on packing and storage, etc. Price risk is another major constituent associated with all modes of international trade

3. Exporter Risk

The chances of exporting inferior quality goods are very high in international trade. Banks need to be vigilant in finding out as much possible whereabouts of the exporter with the help of status reports and other confidential information.

4. Country Risk

Country risks are the risks which are mainly associated with the political and economic conditions of a nation. To rectify this issue, most of the banks have a specialized unit which regulates the level of exposure that the bank will stipulate for each country.

5. Foreign exchange risk

Foreign exchange risk is another major sensitive risk associated with the banks. As the transactions occur in terms of in foreign currency, the traders depend a lot on the exchange rate fluctuations.

General Risks in Letters of Credit:

The following are the general risks which are associated with the letter of credit transactions:

1. Country Risk (Political Risk):

Country risk arises in the situation where the date of repayment is due and the importing Country has modified its export regulations, which makes it impossible for the issuing bank to honour the transaction.

2. Fraud Risk:

This risk occurs when the beneficiary of a letter of credit transaction prepares fake documents, which looks fair and complying, and presents it to the issuing bank. As the documents seem to be good on their face, the issuing bank may honour the presentation and the buyer is obliged to pay to the issuing bank for the goods that he is never going to receive.

3. Risks to the Applicant:

In every letter of credit transaction, the main risk factors for the importer are non-delivery of goods, receipt of goods with inferior quality, exchange rate risk and the bankruptcy risk of the issuing bank.

4. Risks to the Beneficiary:

Another main risk factor in a letter of credit transaction is the inability of the beneficiaries to comply with letter of credit conditions, counterfeit LC, issuing bank's failure risk and issuing bank's country risk.

5. Risks to the Banks:

Letter of credit transactions are risky for every bank as there is chance for non-payment by the applicant, furnishing of fake documents by the beneficiary and changes in export - import regimes of nations and the forex fluctuations.

Module 3

Bill of Lading

Date:	**BILL OF LADING**	Page 1 of _______

SHIP FROM

Name:

Address:

City/State/Zip:

SID#:   FOB: ☐

Bill of Lading Number:_______________

BAR CODE SPACE

SHIP TO

Name: Location #:_____

Address:

City/State/Zip:

CID#:   FOB: ☐

CARRIER NAME: ________________________

Trailer number:

Seal number(s):

SCAC:

Pro number:

BAR CODE SPACE

THIRD PARTY FREIGHT CHARGES BILL TO:

Name:

Address:

City/State/Zip:

SPECIAL INSTRUCTIONS:

Freight Charge Terms: *(freight charges are prepaid unless marked otherwise)*

Prepaid _______   Collect _______   3rd Party _______

☐ (check box)   Master Bill of Lading: with attached underlying Bills of Lading

CUSTOMER ORDER INFORMATION

CUSTOMER ORDER NUMBER	# PKGS	WEIGHT	PALLET/SLIP Y or N	ADDITIONAL SHIPPER INFO
GRAND TOTAL				

CARRIER INFORMATION

HANDLING UNIT		PACKAGE		WEIGHT	H.M. (X)	COMMODITY DESCRIPTION *Commodities requiring special or additional care or attention in handling or stowing must be so marked and packaged as to ensure safe transportation with ordinary care. See Section 2(e) of NMFC Item 360*	LTL ONLY	
QTY	TYPE	QTY	TYPE				NMFC #	CLASS
								RECEIVING STAMP SPACE
						GRAND TOTAL		

Where the rate is dependent on value, shippers are required to state specifically in writing the agreed or declared value of the property as follows:

"The agreed or declared value of the property is specifically stated by the shipper to be not exceeding

_______ per _______ .

COD Amount: $_______________

Fee Terms: Collect: ☐   Prepaid: ☐

Customer check acceptable: ☐

NOTE Liability Limitation for loss or damage in this shipment may be applicable. See 49 U.S.C. - 14706(c)(1)(A) and (B).

RECEIVED, subject to individually determined rates or contracts that have been agreed upon in writing between the carrier and shipper, if applicable, otherwise to the rates, classifications and rules that have been established by the carrier and are available to the shipper, on request, and to all applicable state and federal regulations.

The carrier shall not make delivery of this shipment without payment of freight and all other lawful charges.

_______________ **Shipper Signature**

SHIPPER SIGNATURE / DATE

This is to certify that the above named materials are properly classified, packaged, marked and labeled, and are in proper condition for transportation according to the applicable regulations of the DOT.

Trailer Loaded:
☐ By Shipper
☐ By Driver

Freight Counted:
☐ By Shipper
☐ By Driver/pallets said to contain
☐ By Driver/Pieces

CARRIER SIGNATURE / PICKUP DATE

Carrier acknowledges receipt of packages and required placards. Carrier certifies emergency response information was made available and/or carrier has the DOT emergency response guidebook or equivalent documentation in the vehicle. *Property described above is received in good order, except as noted.*

A bill of lading is a legal document that proves that a carrier has received the goods from a shipper and has agreed to transport them to a certain destination. A bill of lading also shows who owns the goods and can claim them when they are delivered. A bill of lading is important for international trade and logistics because it helps to prevent fraud and disputes.

Types of Bill of lading

A bill of lading is a document that shows the type, amount, and destination of the goods that a carrier is transporting. It also acts as a proof of delivery and a contract for the shipment. There are different kinds of bills of lading, depending on how the goods are transported, how they are delivered, and what their condition is.

Here are some common kinds of bill of lading

1. **Straight bill of lading**

    This is a document that cannot be transferred to someone else and that names the consignee (the person or company who will get the goods). The carrier will only give the goods to the consignee or someone they authorize. This kind of bill of lading is usually used for shipments that are paid in advance or that do not need a change of ownership.

2. **Ocean bill of lading**

    This is a document that is used for shipments by sea. It can be either transferable or non-transferable, depending on whether it is made to order or to a named consignee.

A transferable ocean bill of lading can be signed by the shipper or the consignee to give the ownership of the goods to someone else. A non-transferable ocean bill of lading cannot be given to someone else and only acts as a proof of delivery and a contract.

3. Order bill of lading

This is a document that can be transferred to someone else and that is made to the order of the shipper or a third party. The carrier will give the goods to whoever has the original bill of lading or a valid signature. This kind of bill of lading is usually used for shipments that need a change of ownership or payment on delivery.

4. Multimodal bill of lading

This is a document that covers the transportation of goods by more than one way of transport, such as road, rail, air, or sea. It shows the origin, destination, and intermediate points of the shipment, as well as the duties and risks of each carrier involved. This kind of bill of lading is usually used for international shipments that need multiple carriers.

5. Negotiable bill of lading

This is a document that can be transferred to someone else by signing or delivering it. The carrier will give the goods to the owner of the original bill of lading or a valid signature. This kind of bill of lading is usually used for shipments that involve a sale of goods or a letter of credit.

6. Non-negotiable bill of lading

This is a document that cannot be transferred to someone else. The carrier will give the goods to the consignee or someone they authorize. This kind of bill of lading is usually used for shipments that do not involve a sale of goods or a letter of credit.

7. Claused bill of lading

This is a document that shows that the goods were damaged or defective when the carrier received them or during the transportation. The carrier will write the nature and extent of the damage or defect on the bill of lading and may reduce or deny their responsibility for the loss or damage. This kind of bill of lading is also called a dirty bill of lading or a foul bill of lading.

8. Clean bill of lading

This is a document that shows that the goods were in good condition when the carrier received them and that there were no differences between the description of the goods and the actual goods. The carrier will not make any comments or reservations on the bill of lading and will take full responsibility for the loss or damage of the goods. This kind of bill of lading is also called a clean bill of lading or a fair bill of lading.

9. Open bill of lading

An Open bill of lading is a kind of bill of lading that lets the consignee (the person or entity who gets the goods) to change the ownership of the goods to another party by signing the document. This means that the consignee can trade or transfer the goods to someone else while they are on the way. An open bill of lading is also called a negotiable bill of lading, because it can be negotiated or exchanged like a financial instrument. An open bill of lading is usually used when the goods are shipped on credit or when the consignee wants to have more options in handling the goods.

10. Freight bill of lading

This is a kind of bill of lading that is used for moving goods by land, such as by truck or rail. It is a document that gives the details of the shipment, such as the shipper, the carrier, the consignee, the description of the goods, the weight, the value, and the terms of delivery. It also acts as a proof for the goods and a contract of carriage between the shipper and the carrier. A freight bill of lading can be either negotiable or non-negotiable, depending on whether the ownership of the goods can be transferred to another party or not.

A freight bill of lading usually contains the following information:

- Names and addresses of the sender and the receiver

- Pickup date

- Description of the goods, including quantity, weight, dimensions, value, and freight class

- NMFC code, which is a standardized code that classifies the type and features of the goods

- Additional services, such as liftgate, inside delivery, residential delivery, etc.

- Special instructions, such as delivery appointments, hazardous materials, etc.

- Terms of the shipment, such as prepaid, collect, or third party

- BOL number, which is a unique identifier for the shipment

A freight bill of lading is important for several reasons, such as:

1. It shows the ownership and delivery of the goods.

2. It helps the carrier to bill the shipper and the consignee for the transportation services.

3. It helps the shipper and the consignee to track the status and location of the goods.

4. It helps the shipper and the consignee to file claims in case of loss, damage, or delay of the goods.

5. It helps the shipper and the consignee to follow the customs and regulatory requirements of the origin and destination countries.

Electronic Bill of Lading

An electronic bill of lading (eB/L) is a digital form of a conventional shipping document that acts as a proof of goods transported by a carrier, usually by sea or air. It shows the contract of carriage and the delivery terms.

An eB/L has the same legal status and roles as a paper bill of lading, but it is more effective, secure, and eco-friendly. It can lower the time, cost, and risk of mistakes involved in the exchange of information and documents between the shipper, the carrier, the consignee, and other parties in the supply chain.

Some of the benefits of using an electronic bill of lading are:

1. It can save time and money by cutting down the need for printing, mailing, and storing paper documents.

2. It can enhance the quality and dependability of the information and data shared between the parties involved in the shipment.

3. It can boost the security and traceability of the document and the cargo by using encryption, digital signatures, and blockchain technology.

4. It can lessen the environmental impact of the shipping process by saving paper, ink, and energy.

5. It can ease the compliance with customs and regulatory requirements by providing quicker and simpler access to the document and the data it contains.

6. It can provide more flexibility and convenience for the parties involved in the shipment by allowing them to access, modify, and transfer the document electronically.

However, there are also some obstacles and drawbacks of using an eB/L, such as:

1. Lack of standardization and interoperability among different platforms and systems Legal ambiguity and variability among different countries and jurisdictions.

2. Resistance to change and adoption by some stakeholders and customers.

3. Need for technical infrastructure and support to ensure reliability and availability.

4. Potential cyberattacks and data breaches that could compromise the document and the cargo.

Therefore, an eB/L is a promising innovation that can improve the shipping process, but it also requires careful consideration and collaboration among the parties involved to ensure its effectiveness and legality.

Freight on Board contracts

FOB contracts are a kind of international trade agreement that defines the duties and risks of the seller and the buyer in moving goods by sea or air. FOB means Free on Board, which means that the seller pays for the price of the goods and the loading fees to the departure port. The buyer organizes the shipment and the insurance. The seller is liable for the goods until they are loaded on board the ship, where the risk is passed to the buyer. The buyer then pays for the freight fees, the insurance, and the customs duties, taxes, and other charges to clear the goods and take delivery.

Cost Insurance Freight contracts

CIF contracts are a kind of sale of goods contract in which the seller pays for the cost, insurance, and freight of delivering the goods to the buyer's chosen port. CIF, which is one of the Incoterms, was developed by the International Chamber of Commerce (ICC). CIF contracts mean that the seller arranges and pays for the shipment and the insurance of the goods by sea or waterway to the destination port. The seller is liable for the goods until they arrive at the destination port, where the risk is passed to the buyer. The buyer then pays for the customs duties, taxes, and other charges to clear the goods and take delivery.

Difference between FOB and CIF contracts

FOB contracts	CIF contracts
Free on Board	Cost, Insurance, and Freight
The seller pays for the cost of the goods and the loading charges to the departure port.	The seller pays for the cost of the goods, the insurance, and the freight charges to the destination port.
The buyer arranges the shipment and the insurance.	The seller arranges the shipment and the insurance.
The seller is responsible for the goods until they are loaded on board the ship, where the risk is transferred to the buyer.	The seller is responsible for the goods until they reach the destination port, where the risk is transferred to the buyer.

The buyer pays for the freight charges, the insurance, and the customs duties, taxes, and other fees to clear the goods and take delivery.	The buyer pays for the customs duties, taxes, and other fees to clear the goods and take delivery.
FOB contracts are generally more cost-effective for the buyer, as they have more control over the shipping and insurance options.	CIF contracts are generally more expensive for the buyer, as the seller may charge higher fees to cover their expenses and profits.
FOB contracts are more transparent, as the buyer can track the status and location of the goods.	CIF contracts are less transparent, as the buyer may rely on the seller's information and documentation.
FOB contracts are usually used for bulk or low-value goods, or when the buyer has a preferred carrier or insurer.	CIF contracts are usually used for high-value goods, or when the seller has a preferred carrier or insurer.

Rights and duties of buyer in FOB contracts

Rights	Duties
The buyer can decide which carrier and transportation route to use.	Paying for the goods as per the sales agreement.
The buyer can check the goods for quality and quantity before they are put on the ship	Making arrangements for the main carriage, as well as for the discharge and onward carriage

The buyer can demand money or other remedies from the seller if the goods are not as per the contract terms.	Clearing import formalities, as well as paying relevant duties
The buyer can refuse to accept the goods if they are faulty or different from the contract.	Paying the pre-shipment the for time of import for inspection at clearance.
The buyer can protect the goods with insurance during the journey and get the money back from the insurer if the goods are harmed or lost.	Arranging, as well as paying for insurance.

Rights and duties of Seller in FOB contracts

Rights	Duties
The seller is entitled to get the money for the goods according to the sales contract.	Making the invoice of the goods sold and sending the goods to the port of shipment.
The seller can select the ship, unless the parties have a different agreement.	Getting a contract of carriage under which the goods are delivered at the destination agreed by the contract.

The seller can pass the ownership (title) and the risk of damage or loss of the goods to the buyer when the goods are loaded on the ship chosen by the buyer.	Insuring the goods and getting the insurance policy and delivering the shipping documents to the buyer.
The seller can demand compensation from the buyer if the buyer does not name a ship or give the required documents or directions for the shipment.	Putting the goods on the ship chosen by the buyer, at the port of shipment named in the contract.
The seller can keep a legal claim on the goods until the buyer pays, unless the seller has given the bill of lading to the buyer.	Taking care of the export customs formalities. Paying the expense of loading the goods on the ship. Obtaining a clean bill of lading from the shipping company.

Rights and duties of buyer in CIF contracts

Rights	Duties
The right to have delivery of goods at the named port of destination.	The duty to accept the goods and pay the price as per the contract terms.

The right to reject the goods and cancel the contract if they do not conform to the contract specifications or quality standards and the seller fails to deliver the goods within the agreed time or breaches any other essential term of the contract.	The duty to make arrangements for the unloading, clearance, and onward carriage of the goods at the port of destination.
The right to examine the goods before or after delivery to verify their quantity, quality, and condition and to sue the seller for specific performance if the seller refuses to deliver the goods or delivers goods that are substantially different from the contract.	The duty to pay the import duties, taxes, and other charges related to the importation of the goods.
The right to claim damages from the seller if the goods are lost or damaged during transit or if the seller delivers defective or non-conforming goods.	The duty to provide the seller with the necessary information and documents for the shipment of the goods, such as the name of the ship, the port of destination, and the letter of credit.

The right to take insurance for the goods during transit and to claim from the insurance company in case of any loss or damage to the goods.	The duty to notify the seller of any defects or non-conformities in the goods within a reasonable time after delivery or inspection.
The right to sue the seller for recovery of the price if the seller fails to deliver the documents or the documents are defective or fraudulent and to claim interest from the seller if the seller delays the delivery of the goods or the documents.	The duty to mitigate the loss or damage to the goods if possible and to cooperate with the seller and the insurance company in case of any claim.

Rights and duties of Seller in CIF contracts

Rights	Duties
The right to receive the payment for the goods as per the contract terms.	The duty to arrange for the export customs clearance and pay the export duties and taxes and the duty to deliver the goods and the documents conforming to the contract description and quality standards.
The right to choose the ship, unless otherwise agreed by the parties.	The duty to contract for the carriage of the goods to the named port of destination and pay the freight charges.

The right to transfer the property (title) and risk of loss or damage of the goods to the buyer once the goods are delivered on board of the nominated ship.	The duty to contract for the insurance of the goods during transit and pay the insurance premium.
The right to claim damages from the buyer if the buyer fails to pay the price or accept the documents or the goods.	The duty to obtain a clean bill of lading from the shipping company and provide it to the buyer.
The right to retain a lien on the goods until the payment is made by the buyer, unless the seller has endorsed the bill of lading to the buyer.	The duty to notify the buyer of the shipment details and the expected arrival date of the goods and the duty to mitigate the loss or damage to the goods if possible and to cooperate with the buyer and the insurance company in case of any claim.

The Concept of high seas

The high seas are the areas of the ocean that no country has authority over. They make up about two-thirds of the ocean's surface and are available to all nations for sailing, fishing, research, and other activities. The high seas are regulated by international law, especially the United Nations Convention on the Law of the Sea (UNCLOS), which sets out the rights and obligations of states in using the ocean.

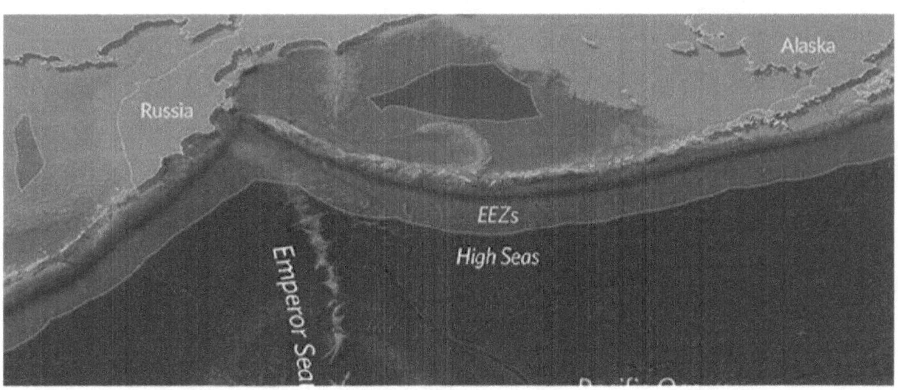

The idea of the high seas goes back to the 17th century, when the Dutch lawyer Hugo Grotius suggested the idea of the freedom of the seas, meaning that the ocean should not belong to any country and should be open to all nations. This idea was opposed by some sea powers, such as Great Britain and Spain, who claimed special rights over large parts of the ocean. However, the freedom of the seas slowly became accepted as a principle of international law in the 19th and 20th centuries, as more nations had maritime interests and trade.

The high seas are not entirely without rules, however. There are laws and regulations that govern the activities and behavior of states and individuals on the high seas, such as the prevention of piracy, the protection of marine environment, the conservation of living resources, the peaceful resolution of disputes, and the cooperation in scientific research. These laws and regulations are based on treaties, conventions, resolutions, and customary law that have been created and adopted by the international community over the years.

The high seas also face some challenges and issues in the 21st century, such as the development of new technologies, the growing demand for resources, the effect of climate change, the risk of terrorism, and the need for better governance and cooperation. These challenges and issues require the modification and development of the existing legal framework and the involvement and coordination of all stakeholders, including states, international organizations, civil society, and private sector.

United Nations Convention on the Law of the Sea (UNCLOS)

The United Nations Convention on the Law of the Sea is an international treaty that establishes the rules and guidelines for the use and protection of the oceans and seas. It specifies the rights and obligations of different countries in relation to the ocean resources, navigation, environment, security, and dispute resolution.

UNCLOS was agreed upon in 1982 after nine years of negotiations among more than 150 countries. It entered into force in 1994

and has been ratified by 168 parties, including 167 states and the European Union. It is regarded as the "constitution of the oceans" and the most comprehensive and authoritative legal framework for the governance of the oceans.

UNCLOS splits the ocean into different zones, such as the territorial sea, the contiguous zone, the exclusive economic zone, the continental shelf, the high seas, and the international seabed area. Each zone has different rules and regulations regarding the sovereignty, jurisdiction, and rights of the coastal and other states. UNCLOS also creates various institutions and mechanisms to assist the implementation and enforcement of the treaty, such as the International Tribunal for the Law of the Sea, the International Seabed Authority, and the Commission on the Limits of the Continental Shelf.

Module 4

Letter of Credit Discounting

A discounted letter of credit is a short-term credit granted by a bank to a beneficiary. The bank purchases documents and invoices from the seller (beneficiary) after fully meeting the conditions and providing the necessary documents to send to the bank to open the LC.

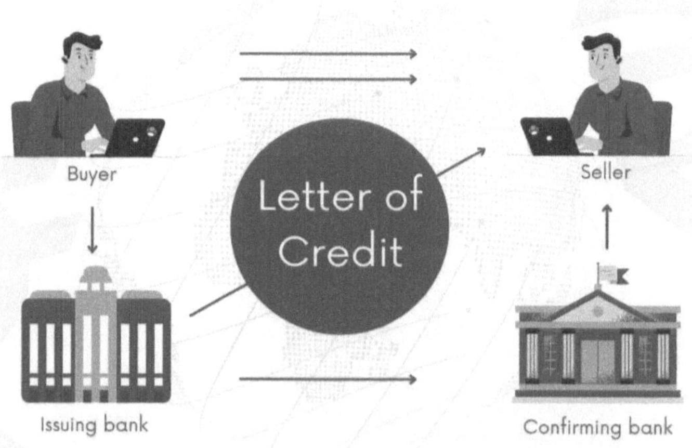

Invoice Discounting/Bill discounting

Invoice discounting can be defined as the advance sale of invoices to an intermediary (invoice discounting company) before maturity. This results in less administrative costs, fees and interest.

Advantages of invoice discounting

1. **Reduction of bad debts**

   Invoice discounting helps reduce the risk of bad debts as the risk of default or non-payment on the part of the buyer/importer is minimized by intermediaries.

2. **Smooth Cash Flow**

   This allows the seller to improve cash inflow and thus avoid cash flow crunch during the transaction.

3. **Low interest rates**

   Usually, invoice discounting service is provided at lower interest rates/fees compared to other premium facilities, so it is beneficial for the seller.

4. **Expedited Processing**

   Since the bill of exchange is a negotiable/exchangeable instrument and can be further rediscounted by the central bank or sold to other financial institutions, it is processed expeditiously. This way, the seller will be able to save money immediately.

5. **Interest**

The seller/beneficiary only has to pay interest on the amount used, unlike other commercial loans.

Disadvantages of invoice discounting

1. **Reduced profits:**

One possible disadvantage of invoice financing is the interest and processing fees that come with any business financing. In the short term, businesses may see a decrease in profits on financed invoices.

However, growth prospects and quick access to liquidity often outweigh this disadvantage.

2. **Industry perspective:**

Some stakeholders disapprove of heavy reliance on invoice financing. But like any business loan product, invoice financing is a means to an end, not a means in itself. A prudent company understands this reality and balances its borrowing while strengthening its internal credit policies.

3. **Loans on commercial invoices only:**

Due to the unsecured nature of this method, commercial invoices. This can be detrimental to businesses that deal with the public and want to raise capital through invoice financing.

4. **Unstable:**

Invoice financing only provides partial or full financing of existing receivables and therefore may not be sufficient if the business is looking for a specific business loan.

5. **Small businesses may have difficulty accessing credit:**

Invoice discounting is generally an option for businesses with significant turnover.

Therefore, one of the disadvantages of this form of financing is that small businesses may have difficulty finding lenders willing to accept them.

6. **Higher costs:**

Because invoice discounting is a short-term loan, invoice discounting often comes with higher costs and fees than traditional bank loans or overdrafts.

7. **Increased reliance on invoice discounting:**

The goal of invoice discounting has always been to manage cash flow strategically and keep the overall success of the business in mind. Businesses can also be stuck in a cycle of debt, unable to operate. There is no existence of monthly cash flow agreements.

8. **Difficulty finding additional business financing:**

Some forms of business financing use accounts receivable as part of the loan security, an invoice discounting arrangement exists (in then the bill becomes the property of the finance company and not your own), which may prevent you from obtaining additional financing.

Invoice discounting process

- Seller/exporter sells goods or services and issues invoice to buyer/importer.

- Buyer receives the goods and signs/accepts the issued invoice. This means that the buyer is obliged to pay the full amount stated on the invoice to the seller before the due date.

- The seller contacts his bank or financial institutions regarding the bill of exchange accepted by the buyer for discounting.

- Banks examine bills of exchange and assess related risks according to their standards.

- Finally, the bank will transfer the money to the seller's account after deducting fees/interest.

- After the deadline, the seller's bank receives the entire amount from the buyer's/buyer's bank.

When can LC be discounted?

LC discounting is a credit facility that is provided by the seller's bank to the exporter. It is a short-term credit facility that can be availed in the following scenarios :

- When an exporter needs immediate payment for their shipment, they can request for discounting of the bills backed by a received letter of credit.

- When an importer wants to extend the payment term, but the exporter requires immediate payment.

- In case an importer fails to pay the money on the due date.

Basic documents needed for LC discount (or LC invoice discount)

- Letter of credit from the importer

- Bill of exchange

- Commercial invoice and packing list

- Documents of title to goods evidencing the dispatch of goods or proof of delivery of goods.

- Discounting request letter

- A bill of lading by the shipping line. Since LC discounting is almost always a type of post shipment finance service.

LC discount limit

Process that the company must follow to request the bank to limit discount for LC invoice:

- First, the beneficiary must register the necessary facilities with the explanation support that request and submit financial documents.

- Bank officials then conduct personal interviews with the exporter.

- The Bank's field investigation team visits the applicant's location for verification.

- The bank checks the applicant's credit score.

- The bank further analyses various parameters of business operations such as history, nature of business operations, business experience, financial viability, etc.

- Thereafter, the applicant's file is opened for sanction by the competent authority.

Working of letter of credit discounting

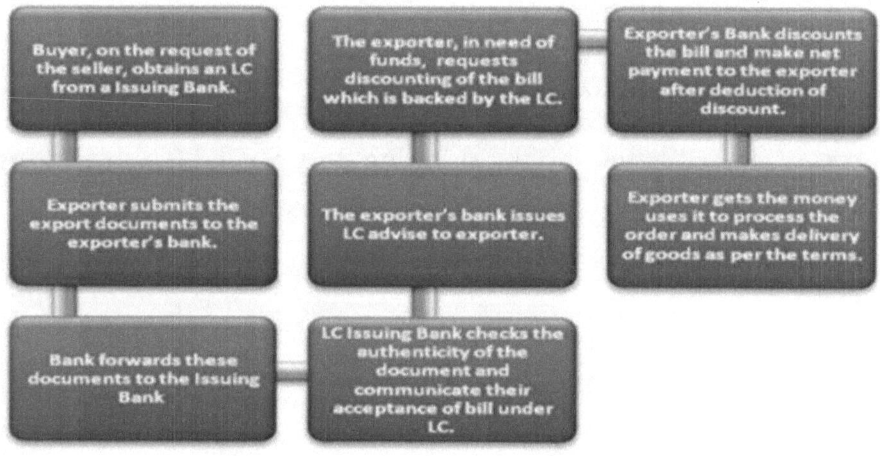

Module 5

Foreign Exchange

Forex is the term used for changing one nation's money into another's. A currency's worth depends upon how much people want to buy, sell, invest, or travel with it, and how the country is doing in the world. For example, right now, 1 US Dollar is equal to 83.22 Indian Rupees.

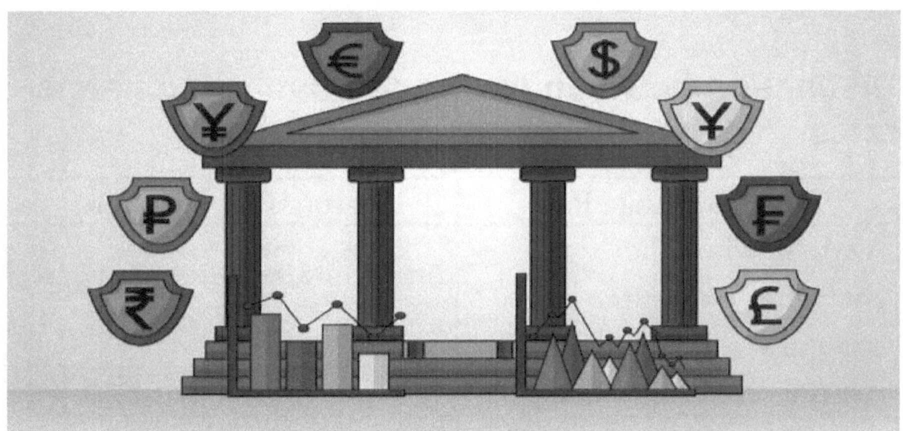

Forex, FX, or currency market is a worldwide decentralized or over-the-counter (OTC)market where people trade different kinds of money. This market sets the price of each currency in relation to others. It covers everything that has to do with buying, selling and swapping money at the current or agreed-upon prices.

An exchange rate tells how much of another country's currency one can get with one unit of his domestic currency. It shows how many euros, pounds, or yen one can buy with one rupee.

When a government or central bank sets the official currency exchange rate to match another country's currency or the gold price, it is called a fixed exchange rate. The goal of a fixed exchange rate system is to maintain a stable value for the currency.

The currency price of a country is determined by the forex market based on how much it is demanded and supplied compared to other currencies. This is called a floating exchange rate. It is different from a fixed exchange rate, where the government has full or partial control over the rate.

Distinction between fixed and floating exchange rates

Fixed Exchange Rate	Floating Exchange Rate
A system where the government or central bank sets and maintains the official currency exchange rate to another country's currency or the price of gold.	A system where the currency price of a country is determined by the supply and demand of the currency in the foreign exchange market.
Stable price	Flexible price

The government or central bank has to buy and sell its own currency on the foreign exchange market to keep the exchange rate stable.	The currency price can fluctuate freely according to the changes in the market conditions.
A fixed exchange rate can create a stable atmosphere for foreign investment, but it also requires a high level of foreign reserves and may cause balance of payment problems	A floating exchange rate can adjust automatically to the market forces, but it also exposes the country to exchange rate risk and volatility

A direct quote is a foreign exchange rate expressed in terms of how much domestic currency is required to purchase one unit of the foreign currency. The foreign currency is usually the U.S. dollar (USD) in forex markets. For example, Rs. 83.22 = 1 USD means that one needs 83.22 rupees to buy one dollar.

An indirect quote is a foreign exchange rate that shows how much foreign currency is needed to purchase or sell one unit of the domestic currency. It is also called a "quantity quotation" because it shows the quantity of foreign currency that can be exchanged for a unit of the domestic currency. For example, Re. 1 = 0.012016 USD means that one rupee can buy 0.012016 dollars.

Theories of exchange rate determination

Some of the most common theories that explain how the foreign exchange market sets the exchange rates between different currencies are:

1. **The Purchasing Power Parity Theory (PPP):** This theory explains that the exchange rate between two currencies is the same as the ratio of their buying power. This means that the exchange rate shows the relative costs of goods and services in different countries. This theory also says that if one country has a higher inflation rate than another, its currency will lose value to keep the buying power equal.

2. **The Interest Rate Parity Theory (IRP):** This theory states that the exchange rate between two currencies is based on the difference in their interest rates. This means that the exchange rate shows the relative trade-off of holding money in different countries. This theory also says that if one country has a higher interest rate than another, its currency will gain value to attract more capital.

3. **The International Fisher Effect (IFE) Theory:** This theory implies that the exchange rate between two currencies is based on the difference in their expected inflation rates. This means that the exchange rate shows the relative expected change in the value of money in different countries. This theory also says that if one country has a higher expected inflation rate than another, its currency will lose value to make up for the loss of purchasing power.

4. **The Unbiased Forward Rate Theory (UFR):** This theory describes that the forward exchange rate between two currencies is a good estimate of the future spot exchange rate. This means that the forward exchange rate shows what the market expects the future spot exchange rate to be. This

theory also says that there is no consistent profit or loss from using forward contracts.

These are some of the main theories of how exchange rates are determined. However, there are also other things that can affect the exchange rate, such as supply and demand, market mood, political and economic events, guessing, interference, etc.

Functions of foreign exchange market

The forex market is a worldwide market that lets participants buy, sell, swap, and bet on currencies. The forex market has several roles that are important for society and the economy. Some of the main functions are:

1. **Transfer function:** This function allows the transfer of money or foreign currencies from one country to another for the payment of goods and services. It involves the change of one currency to another at the current exchange rate. For example, if an Indian importer purchases goods from a US exporter and pays in dollars, the forex market will help the conversion of rupees to dollars.

2. **Credit function:** The forex market gives short-term credit to the importers and exporters to make the flow of goods and services across countries easier. It involves the use of credit tools, such as bank drafts, bills of exchange, and letters of credit.

3. **Hedging function**: The hedging function protects the participants themselves from foreign exchange risks by fixing a future exchange rate for their deals. It involves the

use of derivative tools, such as forward contracts, futures contracts, options contracts, and swaps contracts.

4. **Speculation function:** This function lets the participants make money from the changes in the exchange rates by predicting the future trends of the currencies. It involves the buying and selling of currencies based on market expectations and sentiments.

Transactions in foreign exchange market

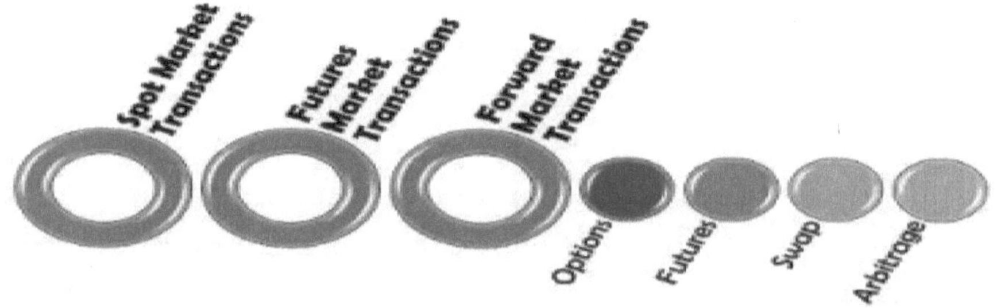

The forex market is a global market that allows participants to buy, sell, swap, and bet on currencies. The forex market has several roles that are important for society and the economy. Some of the main functions are:

1. **Spot Transactions**: This is the quickest way to exchange currencies. Spot transactions mean the exchange or payment of the currencies by the buyer and seller within two days of the deal without a contract. The Spot Exchange Rate is the current exchange rate in the market.

2. **Future Transactions**: These are also transactions that involve contracts like forward transactions. But in future transactions, the contracts have to follow standard rules

about features, date, and size. Regular forward transactions can be changed according to the needs of the parties. In future transactions, a first margin is set and used as security to start a future position.

3. **Forward Transactions**: These are transactions that will happen in the future when the buyer and seller agree to buy and sell currency after 90 days. The agreement is based on a fixed exchange rate for a specific date in the future. The rate that the deal is based on is called the Forward Exchange Rate.

4. **Option Transactions:** These are when an investor can change currency from one type to another at a fixed rate on a certain date. Every investor has the right to convert the currency but is not obliged to do it.

5. **Swap Transactions**: These are when two investors lend and borrow two different currencies at the same time. One investor borrows a currency and pays back in another currency to the other investor. Swap transactions are used to clear debts without facing a foreign exchange risk.

6. **Arbitrage:** These are when different currencies are bought and sold in the forex market to make profits from these deals. They are called arbitrage.

Difference between futures and forwards

Future Contract	Forward Contract
A standardized contract that is traded on an exchange	A customized contract that is traded over the counter (OTC)
The contract terms are fixed and cannot be changed	The contract terms can be negotiated and modified
The contract is settled daily based on the market price	The contract is settled only at the end based on the agreed price
The contract has low risk of default as the exchange acts as a guarantor	The contract has high risk of default as there is no intermediary or regulation
The contract requires an initial margin and a maintenance margin as collateral	The contract does not require any collateral
The contract has high liquidity and transparency	The contract has low liquidity and transparency

Options

Options contracts are contracts that give the buyer the right, but not the duty, to buy or sell an underlying asset at a fixed price on or before a certain date. A call option gives the holder the right to buy a stock and a put option gives the holder the right to sell a stock. Put options are a kind of option that goes up in value as a stock goes down. A put option lets the owner set a price to sell a specific stock, while put sellers agree to buy the stock at that price.

Parties in foreign exchange market

The foreign exchange market is the place where different currencies are bought and sold. The people who take part in this market are:

1. **Central Bank:** The central bank controls the exchange rates and the money supply of its own currency.

2. **Commercial Banks**: The commercial banks act as the agents of forex transactions, helping international trade and exchange and making foreign investments.

3. **Traditional Users:** The traditional users are foreign tourists, companies, patients, and students who need to exchange currencies for their purposes.

4. **Traders and Speculators:** The traders and speculators are the ones who try to make money by trading on short-term market changes.

5. **Brokers:** The brokers are the financial experts who connect the dealers and the investors and offer the best quotes.

Characteristics of forex market

The foreign exchange market has some features that make it unique and important. Some of these features are:

1. **Market Transparency**: It is easy to track the changes in the value of currencies in the forex market through account tracking and real-time portfolio, without the need of brokers.

2. **Dollar is Extensively Traded Currency:** The USD is the most traded currency in the world, as it is paired with almost every country's currency and listed on the forex.

3. **Most Dynamic Market:** The value of the currencies in the forex market changes every second and operates 24 hours a day. This makes it one of the most active markets in the world.

4. **International Network of Dealers:** The foreign exchange market connects the dealers and the customers across the world. There are dealer's institutions located globally to carry out the exchange and trading activities.

5. **"Over-The-Counter" Market:** In different countries, the forex market is highly unregulated and allows over-the-counter trade by the banks through telex and telephone.

6. **High Liquidity:** The currency is the most traded financial instrument across the globe, making the forex market highly liquid.

7. **Twenty-Four Hour Market:** The foreign exchange market works 24 hours a day, enabling active trade and exchange of currencies at any time.

Advantages of Foreign Exchange Market

We know that 'trade makes everyone better-off' and this is also true for exchanging or trading currencies. Some of the benefits of the foreign exchange market are:

1. **High Leverage**: A forex investor can get leverage or loan of up to 20 or 30 times of his/her ability, for trading in the forex market.

2. **International Trade:** Every country has its own currency and so, to make trade easier between two countries, the forex market is needed.

3. **Trading Option:** For the speculators or traders, foreign exchange market is similar to other financial markets where they can earn money on short term changes in the currencies.

4. **Flexibility:** The forex market is open all day and night, and there is no limit on how much or how little one can exchange. It gives flexibility of investment or exchange to the traders.

5. **Hedging Risk:** The forex market helps to hedge the risk of losing money on currency changes while doing global business and trading in foreign currency.

6. **Low Transaction Costs:** Since brokers are not very welcome in the forex market, the transaction cost (called as 'spread') charged by the dealers is quite low compared to other financial markets.

7. **Inflation Control:** To keep the economy stable in the country and control situations like inflation, the central bank keeps a forex reserve which has currencies of different countries around the world. It also uses other ways, like lowering bank lending rates and selling domestic currency for foreign currency.

Disadvantages of trading in forex market

Some of the main disadvantages of trading in the forex market are:

1. **High Volatility:** The foreign exchange market is very unstable, meaning that the exchange rates can vary quickly and unexpectedly due to various things, such as supply and demand, political and economic events, speculation, intervention, etc. This makes it hard for traders to forecast the future trends of the currencies and puts them at high risks of losing money.

2. **Price Determination Process**: The process of setting the exchange rates in the foreign exchange market is very complicated and not clear. The exchange rates are affected by many things, some of which are not visible or measurable. There is no central body or system that regulates or controls the exchange rates. This makes it tough for traders to comprehend and examine the market situations and patterns.

3. **Risk Factor**: The foreign exchange market has a high level of risk for traders, especially for those who use leverage or borrow money to trade. Leverage means that traders can increase their buying power through credit given by brokers or dealers. However, leverage also increases the possible losses if the market goes against the traders' positions. Traders may lose more than their initial investment and may face margin calls or liquidation.

4. **Scammers**: The foreign exchange market is also open to fraud and scams by dishonest brokers, dealers, or other

entities that may change the market or trick the traders. Some of the common scams include fake or unregulated brokers, signal sellers, robot trading, managed accounts, etc. Traders should be cautious and do proper research before picking a broker or a trading platform.

5. **Fear:** The foreign exchange market can also cause fear and stress among traders, especially during times of high volatility or uncertainty. Traders may have emotional changes, such as greed, panic, overconfidence, etc., that may affect their trading choices and performance. Traders should have a definite trading plan and strategy and follow strict risk management rules to avoid emotional trading.

6. **24 X 7 Market:** The foreign exchange market works 24 hours a day and 7 days a week, which may look like an advantage for some traders, but it can also be a disadvantage for others. Traders may have problems in keeping track of the market changes and events across different time zones and regions.

Factors affecting forex market

The factors that affect the forex market are the following:

1. **Inflation Rates:** The changes in inflation in the market affect the exchange rates of currencies. A country that has a lower inflation rate than another will see its currency value go up. The costs of goods and services go up at a slower rate where the inflation is low. A country that has a low inflation rate consistently shows a rising currency value while a country

with high inflation usually sees its currency value go down and has higher interest rates.

2. **Interest Rates**: The changes in interest rate affect the currency value and dollar exchange rate. Forex rates, interest rates, and inflation are all related. Higher interest rates make a country's currency value go up because higher interest rates give higher rates to lenders, which attracts more foreign money, which makes the exchange rates go up.

3. **Country's Current Account / Balance of Payments**: A country's current account shows the balance of trade and earnings on foreign investment. It includes the total number of transactions like its exports, imports, debt, etc. A current account deficit happens when a country spends more of its currency on importing products than it earns from selling exports. This makes the currency value go down. Balance of payments changes the exchange rate of its domestic currency.

4. **Government Debt**: Government debt is public debt or national debt that the central government owes. A country with government debt is less likely to get foreign money, which leads to inflation. Foreign investors will sell their bonds in the open market if they think that a country has too much government debt. This will make the exchange rate value go down.

5. **Terms of Trade**: The terms of trade is related to current accounts and balance of payments and is the ratio of export prices to import prices. A country's terms of trade gets better

if its export prices go up more than its import prices. This results in more income, which makes more demand for the country's currency and makes its currency value go up. This makes the exchange rate go up.

6. **Political Stability & Performance**: A country's political situation and economic performance can affect its currency strength. A country with less political problems is more attractive to foreign investors, which takes away investment from other countries with more political and economic problems. More foreign money makes the domestic currency value go up. A country with good financial and trade policy does not have any doubt in its currency value. But, a country with political troubles may see its exchange rates go down.

7. **Recession**: When a country has a recession, its interest rates are likely to go down, which makes it less likely to get foreign money. As a result, its currency value gets weaker compared to other countries, which lowers the exchange rate.

8. **Speculation**: If investors expect a country's currency value to go up, they will want more of that currency to make money in the near future. As a result, the currency value will go up because of more demand. This also makes the exchange rate go up.

Risks involved in foreign exchange

The foreign exchange market is the place where different currencies are bought and sold. The people who take part in this market face different kinds of risks, such as:

1. **Transaction risk**: This is the risk of losing money because of changes in the exchange rate from the time of the deal to the time of the payment. For example, if a company buys goods from another country and pays in its currency, but the exchange rate changes badly before the payment is done, the company will have to pay more than planned.

2. **Economic risk:** This is the risk of losing market value because of changes in the exchange rate that affect how competitive and profitable a company is. For example, if a company sells its products to another country and the exchange rate changes badly, the company will lose its price edge and may lose customers or market share.

3. **Translation risk**: This is the risk of losing accounting value because of changes in the exchange rate that affect how financial statements are reported. For example, if a company has assets and liabilities in different currencies, and the exchange rate changes badly, the company will have to report lower net worth or higher losses.

4. **Jurisdiction risk:** This is the risk of losing money because of changes in the laws or rules of a country that affect the foreign exchange deals. For example, if a country puts limits on capital or currency movements, or lowers its currency

value, the foreign exchange deals may be stopped or become more expensive.

CURRENCY FORECASTING

Currency forecasting is the process of estimating how the value of one currency will change compared to another. Currency forecasting can assist individuals, businesses, and financial institutions in making smart financial choices. There are various methods of currency forecasting, such as purchasing power parity, relative economic strength, and econometric models. For example, The USD to INR exchange rate is expected to drop from 83.12 rupees per dollar in December 2023 to 82.98 rupees per dollar in January 2024, according to a website that uses historical trends and technical analysis.

Pound/Euro exchange rate forecast 2014 | Foremost Currency Group

Currency forecasting models

1. **Purchasing power parity (PPP):** PPP is the concept that the same goods in different countries should have the same prices, after adjusting for the exchange rate and excluding transaction and shipping costs. PPP predicts that the exchange rate will adjust to balance price changes due to inflation.

2. **Relative economic strength (RES):** RES measures the levels of economic growth across countries to forecast exchange rates. RES assumes that a country with a stronger economy will have a stronger currency, as it will attract more investment and trade.

3. **Econometric models (EM):** EMs use statistical methods to examine a wide range of variables that may influence currency exchange rates, such as interest rates, trade balance, inflation, GDP, etc. EM can be tailored to fit the specific features and movements of different currency pairs.

4. **SARIMA:** This is a kind of econometric model that considers seasonal variations and self-correlation in time series data. SARIMA operates by modelling the connection between previous and present values of a time series and finding patterns in the data.

5. **Machine learning models:** These models use sophisticated algorithms and data mining methods to learn from historical data and make forecasts based on patterns and trends. Machine learning models can take into account a large number of factors and complex interactions that may influence currency exchange rates.

IMF Classification of Exchange Rates

The IMF has a Practical System of Exchange Rate Regimes: The system sorts out exchange rate regimes mainly by how much the exchange rate depends on the market versus official intervention, with market-based rates generally being more adaptable.

The system divides them into four main groups:

Hard pegs (for example, exchange regimes with no own currency and currency board regimes).

Soft pegs (such as fixed exchange regimes, exchange rates within fixed bands, crawling pegs, stabilized regimes, and regimes that crawl like pegs).

Floating regimes (like floating and free floating); and a leftover category, other managed.

Residual category, other managed

1. **Exchange regimes with no own legal tender:** The currency of another country is the only legal tender (officially its dollarization), or the member is part of a monetary or currency union that uses the same legal tender among its members. Such regimes mean that the monetary authorities give up all control over domestic monetary policy.

2. **Currency board regimes:** A monetary system based on a clear legal promise to exchange domestic currency for a certain foreign currency at a fixed exchange rate, along with limits on the issuing authority to make sure it meets its legal duty. This means that domestic currency is only created in

exchange for foreign currency and that it is fully supported by foreign assets, leaving little room for discretionary monetary policy and getting rid of traditional central bank roles, such as monetary regulation and lender-of-last-resort. Some flexibility may still be possible, depending on how rigid the banking rules of the currency board regime are.

3. **Conventional fixed peg regimes**: The country fixes its currency within margins of ±1 percent or less against another currency; a cooperative system, such as the ERM II; or a group of currencies, where the group is made up of the currencies of major trading or financial partners and weights match the geographical spread of trade, services, or capital flows. The currency groups can also be standardized, as in the case of the SDR. There is no promise to keep the parity forever. The exchange rate may change within narrow margins of less than ±1 percent around a central rate — or the highest and lowest value of the exchange rate may stay within a narrow margin of 2 percent for at least three months. The monetary authority keeps the fixed parity through direct or indirect intervention.

4. **Fixed exchange rates within horizontal bands:** The value of the currency is kept within certain margins of change of more than ±1 percent around a fixed central rate or the margin between the highest and lowest value of the exchange rate goes beyond 2 percent. As in the case of conventional fixed pegs, reference may be made to a single currency, a cooperative system, or a currency group. There is a limited

amount of monetary policy choice, depending on the band width.

5. **Crawling pegs:** The currency is changed regularly in small amounts at a fixed rate or in response to changes in specific quantitative measures, such as past inflation differences with major trading partners, differences between the inflation goal and expected inflation in major trading partners. The rate of crawl can be set to adjust for observed inflation or other measures (backward looking), or set at a preannounced fixed rate and/or below the expected inflation differences (forward looking). Keeping a crawling peg limits monetary policy in a way similar to a fixed peg system.

6. **Exchange rates within crawling bands:** The currency is kept within certain margins of change of at least +1 percent around a central rate or the margin between the highest and lowest value of the exchange rate goes beyond 2 percent and the central rate or margins are changed regularly at a fixed rate or in response to changes in specific quantitative measures. The degree of exchange rate flexibility depends on the band width. Bands are either equal around a crawling central parity or widen slowly with an unequal choice of the crawl of upper and lower bands.